"Susan Tassone shares with us the beauty, truth, wisdom, and spirituality found in St. Faustina's *Diary*. Now, with *Day by Day with Saint Faustina*, she hands us 365 theological gems with an original reflection and prayer for each one. This is a tremendous achievement ... and a truly lovely and 'pray-able' prayer book."

— MOST REVEREND ROBERT P. REED
Auxiliary Bishop of Boston

"Susan Tassone's new book is a means to experience God's overwhelming love for each of us. By spending a little time each day reflecting on a bite-sized morsel of the *Diary* of St. Faustina—followed by a very succinct and eye-opening reflection, and then a short prayer—God can change our perspective and our lives through His powerful love. Seeing how God worked in the life of St. Faustina helps us see how He wants to work in our own hearts. This treasure of a book is a wonderful way to develop a very doable habit of ongoing formation. I highly recommend it!"

— FATHER JOSEPH ROESCH, M.I.C.
Vicar General, Rome, Italy

"*Day by Day with Saint Faustina* is a spiritual storehouse—a blessing—that helps you reflect more deeply each day on the writings of this amazing saint and 'friend.' Especially suited to men and women with busy, demanding lives, these quotations, reflections, and prayers will give you a spiritual 'boost' each day of the year."

—MICHELE FAEHNLE
Co-author of *Our Friend Faustina*

"This much-needed introduction to St. Faustina, her spirituality, and God's never-ending mercy is a wonderful choice for those (including me) who have felt a little intimidated by the depth—and length—of the visionary's *Diary*. Here, day by day, author Susan Tassone shares the key themes, beauty, and comfort the *Diary* offers all of us. It's a grace-filled nudge that encourages each of us to read the *Diary* itself."

—FATHER EDWARD LOONEY
Author of *A Heart Like Mary's: 31 Daily Meditations to Help You Live and Love as She Does*

"*Day by Day with Saint Faustina* gives us a wonderful approach to comprehending the infinite Divine Mercy of God. I've long hoped that somebody would be able to open the depths of St. Faustina's spirituality in a way that would allow people to slowly acquire her ability to trust, just as she slowly grew in prayer, in understanding God's will, and eventually in fully trusting in His love."

—Father Dan Cambra, M.I.C.
Holy Souls Sodality
The National Shrine of The Divine Mercy

"*Day by Day with Saint Faustina* is a must-have and must-read companion for your daily prayer life to better discern God's will for you. Here's how to imitate St. Faustina's daily pilgrimage on your own path to a deeper spirituality and closer, more personal, relationship with the Father, Son, and Holy Spirit."

—David M. Carollo
Executive Director, World Apostolate of
Fatima USA—Our Lady's Blue Army

DAY BY DAY
WITH
SAINT FAUSTINA

DAY BY DAY
WITH
SAINT
FAUSTINA

365 Reflections

SUSAN TASSONE

SOPHIA INSTITUTE PRESS
Manchester, New Hampshire

Sophia Institute Press
Box 5284, Manchester, NH 03108
1-800-888-9344
www.SophiaInstitute.com

Sophia Institute Press® is a registered trademark of Sophia Institute.

Library of Congress Cataloging-in-Publication Data
To come.

First printing

*I dedicate this book to the sick, the suffering,
and the dying throughout the world.*

*Know that, always favorites of St. Faustina,
you remain in her prayers.*

*Know that, as we join in those prayers,
you are in ours.*

*Know that, offering up your pain
as such a powerful prayer for others,
the Church thanks you,
your parish thanks you,
your family and friends thank you,
and I thank you.*

We thank you so very much.

CONTENTS

Appendices

A Genuine Aid to Our Daily Prayer

Most Reverend Thomas J. Olmsted
Bishop of Phoenix

As we walk through life in this "valley of tears," we are often beset by trials of various kinds. We experience temptations, the misery of our weaknesses and sinfulness, conflicts with others, misunderstandings, and more. It can be encouraging for us to know that many saints experienced similar struggles, and we can learn much from them about how to navigate the stormy waters of life in this world.

The secret for St. Faustina was constant prayer. We learn from her *Diary* that she brought everything to the Lord in prayer, then listened to Him and received all that He wanted to tell her. In this way, St. Faustina was led day by day and even moment by moment into a deeper relationship with Jesus Christ, the source of her happiness.

She teaches us to do the same.

We often think that our weaknesses and sinfulness make us unworthy of such intimacy with God, but it is just the opposite. Jesus tells us through St. Faustina that "one thing alone is necessary: that the sinner set ajar the door of his heart, be it ever so little, to let in a ray of God's merciful grace, and then God will do the rest" (*Diary*, 1507).

When St. Faustina opened the door of her heart, she was often drawn into the "abyss" of God's mercy. She found great delight in hiding herself in the Lord's "Most Merciful Heart" (*Diary*, 1395). There, she found herself to be "immersed in God" (*Diary*, 495), and this immersion in Him brought her great inner peace, even amid the many sufferings she endured.

This deep communion with the Lord that St. Faustina experienced was not automatic, nor was it easy. Again, it was a result of her dedication to prayer, in which she engaged in a constant conversation with Jesus. As she put it, "Every morning during meditation, I prepare myself for the whole day's struggle" (*Diary*, 91).

What struggles did she face? She faced debilitating illnesses, the hardships of community life, the monotony of the daily routine, and often being misunderstood by her superiors and fellow sisters in the convent.

The Lord would frequently remind her of the need to be united to Him in His suffering. Through prayer, she came to realize that "suffering is a great grace; through suffering the soul becomes like the Savior; in suffering love becomes crystallized; the greater the suffering, the purer the love" (*Diary*, 57). It wasn't just suffering for suffering's sake but, rather, suffering in union with Jesus that brought St. Faustina true joy.

As her union with Jesus deepened, the life of virtue flourished within her. She was able to love all those whom God placed before her, even the most difficult. Embracing the cross and surrendering to God's will in all things led the saint to say, "I have discovered a fountain of happiness in my soul, and it is God" (*Diary*, 887).

The Lord is offering each of us a deep, intimate relationship with Him. The key is to set aside some time each day for prayer, cultivating the silence and solitude necessary for us to be alone with the Lord and to listen to Him.

Susan Tassone's *Day by Day with Saint Faustina* can be a genuine aid to our daily prayer. Every time we pick up this little treasure of a book, we will find the deep wisdom of St. Faustina's *Diary* presented in bite-size pieces, one nugget of wisdom at a time. In her daily reflections, Susan fleshes out the teaching on Divine Mercy in contemporary language, with very helpful images and analogies.

Spending time with the Lord in this way will help us all to taste the joy that St. Faustina experienced as she was "drawn into the bosom of the Most Holy Trinity ... immersed in the love of the Father, the Son and the Holy Spirit" (*Diary*, 1670).

Personal
Acknowledgments

The support and friendship of these men and women is beyond belief. I thank God for each and every one of you. We've been in each other's thoughts and prayers as I wrote this book and because of that, to quote St. Faustina, "our friendship … deepened" (*Diary*, 1171).

To Charlie McKinney: Thank you so much for publishing this, my first book for Sophia Institute Press. Thank you to your staff. I know many books will follow.

To Bill Dodds: My copy editor par excellence. For every book we've done together, I'm so grateful to have you by my side! They're all masterpieces! How St. Faustina is bursting with joy! You're the best.

To Bert Ghezzi: How do I put into words what a friend like you gives? So far above, so far beyond. You've provided invaluable editorial advice. Thank you from "the kid."

To Father Dan Cambra, M.I.C.: You casually point out a word used often in St. Faustina's *Diary* — "purgatory," "conversion," "adoration" — and four books later, here we are. Thank you for those words, and thank you for helping me gain access to using the *Diary* in my work. You've been tremendously supportive in every way.

To Steven Jay Gross: A father and friend to so many a people ... and pups. (Such a lover of animals!) You have made it easier, you have made it possible, for me to move closer to doing God's will. He knows we all need a little help from our friends. That's you, my friend.

To Jackie Lindsey: This is book number twelve together. You're always there, ready to read and give your advice and final blessing, telling me, "You have another masterpiece." Thank you so much, dear Jackie.

To Maria Faber: A true friend takes 365 day-by-day manuscript pages and helps you put them in a logical and pleasing order. That's you! All that, and much more. You have no idea how much you helped me with this book. For this, and for your help on my earlier book, I can never thank you enough.

To Pat Hackett: Where to begin? Your friendship and words of wisdom mean so much to me. You give me peace and joy. Thanks, too, for your sister, Joan. What a cheerleader and a friend!

To Loyola University Chicago librarians Yolande Wersching and Vanessa Crouther: Once again, you stood ready and offered the greatest assistance and support … in your gracious and generous manner. I'm deeply grateful. I look forward to the three of us enjoying heaven together and spending time with St. Faustina, when our work here is done.

Special thanks to the designers of the book cover, Tianna Williams and Garrett Fosco. Your design of a radiant St. Faustina captures her message of hope and mercy.

Beginning Your Own Retreat, Journey, Pilgrimage

It's been an amazing time for me. It's been a retreat. a journey. a pilgrimage, researching and writing *Day by Day with Saint Faustina: 365 Reflections*.

It's been praying *to* her and *with* her so that you can draw closer to her, too.

I'm so pleased and grateful that the result is a book that doesn't have just "a little something for everybody." It has a *lot* of something for all of us, no matter how familiar — or unfamiliar — we are with the *Diary* of this great mystic and visionary.

I'm happy to say it's both a comprehensive introduction to her writing, and a solid answer for those asking how to apply her teaching and example in daily life.

And, no surprise to those familiar with my other books, the holy souls in purgatory are a central part of it, just as they were to St. Faustina.

Day by Day with Saint Faustina, shows her communion *with*, and devotion *to*, them.

She shares the value of suffering and how our daily work — including its smallest activities — can be transformed into a sacrifice for the living and the deceased when offered to God.

St. Faustina writes of the ugliness of sin and how to live out our mission in life now.

Here, page after page, all of us can come to know and better understand the *Diary*'s teachings and major themes, including love, mercy, trust, and humility. Of recognizing, accepting, and living God's will for each of us.

St. Faustina will help you:

- Grow closer to Christ in the Eucharist.

- Develop a stronger, deeper daily prayer life ... with the help of the angels and saints.

- Get along better with others, including those closest to you.

- Apply her "Secrets of Sanctity."

- Trust God more.

- Let the realities of heaven, hell, and purgatory influence your choices now.

- Love the Blessed Mother even more, and let her love draw you closer to her Son.

- Use your suffering to help others, including the souls in purgatory.

- Come to better understand, and take advantage of, the spiritual powerhouse that is the Sacrament of Reconciliation.

- Become a person of mercy by learning from the Saint of Mercy, a woman who spent her life—day by day—teaching others about the infinite love and compassion of God, who is Divine Mercy.

It's my hope, my prayer—for you and for me—that we take St. Faustina's message to heart as we read it, reflect on it, pray it … and live it.

Day by day, with St. Faustina.

—Susan

CHAPTER ONE

Reflections

FOR

January

January 1

A LIFETIME RESOLUTION

My goal is God ... (*Diary*, 775)

Reflection

At the start of a new year most of us have a resolution or two in mind. Then, too, each new year brings us closer to our death ... and an opportunity to reflect on our "life goal." It's an opportunity to consider how—over the next twelve months—we can move closer to it. How will this year be different if, like St. Faustina, I consciously and consistently remind myself that "my goal is God"?

Prayer

Over this year, Dear Lord, help me cling to, and move toward, what really matters; and let go of, and avoid, what truly doesn't.

Jesus, I trust in You.

January 2

INFINITE MERCY AND LOVE

[Jesus said to St. Faustina:] **If I call creatures into being—that is the abyss of My mercy.** (*Diary*, 85)

Reflection

There is something about you that attracted God to create you. You were chosen by God before all creation.

God could have called any soul into being, but He chose you! He wants you and made you for eternal happiness.

Prayer

Thank You, Heavenly Father, for creating me. For choosing me out of Your love and mercy to share all eternity with You.

Jesus, I trust in You.

January 3
A NAME DEAREST TO OUR HEART

The Name of Jesus. Oh, how great is Your Name, O Lord! It is the strength of my soul. When my strength fails, and darkness invades my soul, Your Name is the sun whose rays give light and also warmth, and under their influence the soul becomes more beautiful and radiant, taking its splendor from Your Name. (*Diary*, 862)

Reflection

There's something calming, soothing, comforting in the name of someone dearest to our heart. Just hearing it, just whispering it, can have a physical, emotional, and spiritual effect on us. That was the case for St. Faustina and "Jesus." It can be that way for us, too.

Prayer

Jesus.... Jesus.... Jesus....
   Jesus, I trust in You.

January 4

GETTING TO KNOW YOU

I often ask the Lord Jesus for an intellect enlightened by faith. I express this to the Lord in these words: "Jesus, give me an intellect, a great intellect, for this only that I may understand You better; because the better I get to know You, the more ardently will I love You. (*Diary*, 1474)

Reflection

Not even the sky—not even heaven itself—is the limit when it comes to getting to know God, getting to know all about Him. It can be comforting to realize your Creator made you with the exact amount of intellectual capacity you need to do what He's calling you to do on earth. And to know Him as no one else knows Him when you enter heaven.

Prayer

I want to learn more about you, Lord, from the sacraments, from prayer, from Scripture and books. From time spent alone with You in adoration. I suppose it's "just" human nature, just the nature You've given us, to want to know as much as possible about Someone I love.

Jesus, I trust in You.

January 5
BE LOVING

> Jesus, help me to go through life doing
> good to everyone. (*Diary*, 692)

Reflection

The old joke goes: I love humanity. It's people I can't stand. An old joke with a lot of truth to it. Yes, St. Faustina prayed for everyone—living and dead—but she also had to do good to some in particular: those with whom she lived and that, at times, was not easy. Again, the same holds true for us. Again, we're wise to pray: "Jesus, help me!"

Prayer

Dear Lord, give me patience to be kind to those who are not kind to me. To be kinder to those to whom I am not kind. Choosing to do good to everyone.

Jesus, I trust in You.

January 6

TIPS FOR BEGINNERS

Let [the directress of the novitiate] train the novices in
the practice of humility, because only a humble heart
keeps the vows easily and experiences the great joys that
God pours out upon the faithful soul. (*Diary*, 544)

Reflection

Today's quote is from a section in the *Diary* where St. Faustina
was writing down her advice on starting a new religious order. Her
words for helping novices are really just one word: humility. It's the
foundation for a spiritually successful nun ... husband or wife ...
single person ... priest.... For anyone and everyone.

Prayer

Give me meekness, Lord. Give me humility of heart. Give my soul
the great joys that come from being humble.

Jesus, I trust in You.

January 7

DO NOT BE AFRAID

The Lord visited me today and said, **My daughter, do not be afraid of what will happen to you. I will give you nothing beyond your strength. You know the power of My grace; let that be enough.** (*Diary*, 1491)

Reflection

As Jesus tells St. Faustina, "I will give you nothing beyond your strength." Every life is peppered with a lot of "somethings" that make it challenging, and frightening, but none of them will be beyond what we can handle.

Prayer

Give me courage when I worry about what may happen to me. Give me strength when those hardships come and to remember the power of your grace is enough.

Jesus, I trust in You.

January 8
LIFE'S MOST SOLEMN MOMENT

The most solemn moment of my life is the moment
when I receive Holy Communion. (*Diary*, 1804)

Reflection

One synonym for "solemn" is "awe-inspiring." That fits what St.
Faustina is describing. "Solemn" isn't a word we use very often to
describe our everyday lives. Society, in general, has become much
more casual. But receiving Our Lord in the Eucharist— which can
happen daily as well as weekly—isn't meant to be casual. Shouldn't
be casual. If we prepare for that event, if we pray about that event,
if we step forward knowing we are about to receive the Second
Person of the Blessed Trinity and our Savior, it *will* be profound. It
can become "the most solemn moment of my life."

Prayer

Dear Lord, who am I that my Lord should come to me? Help me
better realize and appreciate what is happening and Who is present
and being offered to me.

Jesus, I trust in You.

January 9
THE SPIRIT OF JESUS

I am greatly surprised at how one can be so jealous. When I see someone else's good, I rejoice at it as if it were mine. The joy of others is my joy, and the suffering of others is my suffering, for otherwise I would not dare to commune with the Lord Jesus. The spirit of Jesus is always simple, meek, sincere; all malice, envy, and unkindness disguised under a smile of good will are clever little devils. A severe word flowing from sincere love does not wound the heart. (*Diary*, 633)

Reflection

Simplicity, meekness, and sincerity. Or malice, envy, and unkindness. The spirit of Jesus. Or that of smiling "clever little devils." Every day the choice is ours.

Prayer

Help me remember, Dear Lord, that: "Love is patient and kind; love is not jealous or boastful; it is not arrogant or rude. Love does not insist on its own way; it is not irritable or resentful; it does not rejoice at wrong, but rejoices in the right" (1 Cor 13: 4–6).

Jesus, I trust in You.

January 10
SO LITTLE, SO MUCH

> Only love has meaning; it raises up our smallest
> actions into infinity. (*Diary*, 502)

Reflection

"Only love has meaning," or as St. Paul put it, "So faith, hope, love
abide, these three; but the greatest of these is love" (1 Cor 13:13).
It's a common adage that "you can't take it with you," but that's
not true. Not the money, power, or prestige. But the love. The love
between us and others, living or dead. The love between God and
us. Love, and our smallest actions of love here on earth, stretch into
the infinite.

Prayer

Dear God, help me abide in love and let Your love abide in me.

Jesus, I trust in You.

January 11
LOVING, DESPITE FEELINGS

[Jesus said to St. Faustina:] **My pupil, have great love for those who cause you suffering. Do good to those who hate you.** I answered, "O my Master, You see very well that I feel no love for them, and that troubles me." Jesus answered, **It is not always within your power to control your feelings. You will recognize that you have love if, after having experienced annoyance and contradiction, you do not lose your peace, but pray for those who have made you suffer and wish them well.** (*Diary*, 1628)

Reflection

Straight from the Savior of the world: "It is not always within your power to control your feelings." We feel what we feel, sometimes despite what we want to feel. But we can choose to do what we do, despite those feelings. We can choose to keep our peace and to pray for others.

Prayer

Thank You for not asking me to do the impossible, Lord. And, maybe more accurately, thank You for helping me accomplish the seemingly impossible because You're with me.

Jesus, I trust in You.

January 12
BELLS AND WHISTLES

Neither graces, nor revelations, nor raptures, nor gifts granted to a soul make it perfect, but rather the intimate union of the soul with God. These gifts are merely ornaments of the soul, but constitute neither its essence nor its perfection. My sanctity and perfection consist in the close union of my will with the will of God. God never violates our free will. It is up to us whether we want to receive God's grace or not. It is up to us whether we will cooperate with it or waste it. (*Diary*, 1107)

Reflection

St. Faustina has surprising—and valuable—advice. Don't get distracted by graces, revelations, raptures, or gifts. They don't make a soul perfect. They're nice "ornaments of the soul" but not "its essence nor its perfection." Want a perfect soul? Focus on closing the gap between your will and God's.

Prayer

Your kingdom come, *Your* will be done. Help me with that, Lord. It's something I really want, and I know You want, too.

Jesus, I trust in You.

January 13
LOVE DEFINED

> The quintessence of love is sacrifice and suffering.
> Truth wears a crown of thorns. Prayer involves the
> intellect, the will, and the emotions. (*Diary*, 1103)

Reflection

Dear St. Faustina didn't sugarcoat it. Sacrifice, suffering, thorns, and work.

Holiness is not for wimps.

Prayer

I can see, Lord, that my personal holiness is absolutely impossible ... without You.

Jesus, I trust in You.

January 14

FROM TODAY ON . . .

In the evening, after the conference, I heard these words: **I am with you. During this retreat, I will strengthen you in peace and in courage so that your strength will not fail in carrying out My designs. Therefore, you will cancel out your will absolutely in this retreat and, instead, My complete will shall be accomplished in you. Know that it will cost you much, so write these words on a clean sheet of paper: "From today on, my own will does not exist," and then cross out the page. And on the other side write these words: "From today on, I do the will of God everywhere, always, and in everything." Be afraid of nothing; love will give you strength and make the realization of this easy.** (*Diary*, 372)

Reflection

What would it be like for me if I did the will of God "everywhere, always, and in everything?" Yes, it sounds like a very good idea, the perfect plan, but ... frightening. Maybe St. Faustina was thinking that too because God quickly added, "Be afraid of nothing; love will give you strength and make the realization of this easy." He says the same to me.

Prayer

Today, Dear Heavenly Father, I want to do Your will. Please, show me how.

Jesus, I trust in You.

January 15
ST. FAUSTINA'S "SOUL ROUTINE"

O my Jesus, you know what efforts are needed to live sincerely and unaffectedly with those from whom our nature flees, or with those who, deliberately or not, have made us suffer. Humanly speaking, this is impossible. At such times more than at others, I try to discover the Lord Jesus in such a person and for this same Jesus, I do everything for such people. In such acts, love is pure, and such practice of love gives the soul endurance and strength. (*Diary*, 766)

Reflection

In today's quote St. Faustina shows us even a saint has trouble living with some people. Those who rub us the wrong way. Those who have hurt us in some way. Faustina shares tips too: Fortify your soul. That is, give it "endurance and strength." We, too, can discover Jesus in such a person. And come to see doing for them is doing for Him. What a concept! What a comfort. What's stopping you from starting your own "soul routine"?

Prayer

Son of God, Pure Love, help me practice acts of love that will give my soul greater endurance and strength.

Jesus, I trust in You.

January 16

THE "MEAT AND POTATOES" OF SPIRITUALITY

> The spiritual life is to be lived earnestly and sincerely. (*Diary*, 388)

Reflection

St. Faustina sounds pretty serious today. "Earnestly." "Sincerely."
Yes, the spiritual life is amazing, incredible, out of this world! But
... it's "meat and potatoes," too. It's hard work that demands —
demands! — dedication, self-sacrifice, and unflinching honesty.
What St. Faustina says time and again throughout her *Diary* is that
it's not just worth it, it's *more* than worth it. It's a taste of heaven on
earth, and a treasure stored up in heaven. Just waiting for you.

Prayer

Help me have, and use, what it takes to constantly deepen, refresh,
and renew my spiritual life, Dear Jesus.

Jesus, I trust in You.

January 17
WITH THEM

I prayed today for a soul in agony, who was dying without the Holy Sacraments, although she desired them. But it was already too late. It was a relative of mine, my uncle's wife. She was a soul pleasing to God. There was no distance between us at that moment. (*Diary*, 207)

Reflection

We're used to so many forms of instant communication but, we know, it's never the same as being there with a loved one in person. Especially if that loved one is seriously ill or near death. In today's quote St. Faustina tells us that through prayer (and in a particular and powerful way through the Divine Mercy Chaplet), we *are* there in person, through the Three Persons of the Blessed Trinity.

Prayer

Gentle Jesus, I join my prayers to St. Faustina's for those who will die today without receiving the sacraments. Divine Mercy, grant them mercy and let them enter Your Kingdom.

Jesus, I trust in You.

January 18

A POOR, YOUNG JESUS

Jesus came to the main entrance today, under the guise of a poor young man. This young man, emaciated, barefoot and bareheaded, and with his clothes in tatters, was frozen because the day was cold and rainy. He asked for something hot to eat.... O my Jesus, now everything is clear to me, and I understand all that has just happened. I somehow felt and asked myself what sort of a poor man is this who radiates such modesty. From that moment on, there was stirred up in my heart an even purer love toward the poor and the needy. (*Diary*, 1312–1313)

Reflection

Most of us probably seldom if ever picture Jesus as a young man in His late teens or His twenties. The Gospels jump from twelve to thirty. St. Faustina took a while to recognize who was at the convent door and then realized what tipped her off: His modesty. How would our lives be different, how would we change, if we truly *loved* the poor and needy of all ages?

Prayer

Lord, help me see You and serve You in all Your disguises.

Jesus, I trust in You.

January 19

SHARING SELF AND HAPPINESS

January 19, 1937.... I feel a certain need to share myself with others. I have discovered a fountain of happiness in my soul, and it is God. (*Diary*, 887)

Reflection

When we have something really good, something from God, we just naturally (supernaturally?) want to pass it on. To share it. That's certainly true for the happiness, the deep and unique joy, that comes from Him. That *is* Him. How to share it? Love — that is, God — will find a way for us. We just have to pay attention.

Prayer

Thank You so much for the joy You bring, Lord. For the joy You share. For those bits of heaven on earth.

Jesus, I trust in You.

January 20
MY GUIDE

Jesus, Life and Truth, my Master, guide every
step of my life,... (*Diary*, 688)

Reflection

Yes, we can offer the same prayer St. Faustina did, but if we are
older than she ever was—dying at age thirty-three—we can pray
a variation of it, too: "guide every *stage* of my life." Whether we're
a child, teen, young adult, middle-ager, or senior, the same Life and
Truth, the same Master, is ready to guide us. He came to earth; He
suffered, died, and rose from the dead ... to lead us home. Step by
step.

Prayer

Be my guide, Dear Jesus, at this stage of my life and through all it
entails. Be my guide.

Jesus, I trust in You.

January 21
FAITHFUL TO PRAYER

Jesus gave me to understand how a soul should be faithful to prayer despite torments, dryness, and temptations, because oftentimes the realization of God's great plans depends mainly on such prayer. If we do not persevere in such prayer, we frustrate what the Lord wanted to do through us or within us. (*Diary*, 872)

Reflection

It's nice to think we have it made once we reach some kind of spiritual plateau that pleases us. But it just isn't so. The old "torments, dryness, and temptations" can return. And new ones can be worse. Then—like putting one foot in front of the other to move ahead—we need to say one prayer after another. To, like Jesus, in our anguish, "pray longer."

Prayer

Help me persevere in prayer, Dear Lord. Especially when You seem distant.

Jesus, I trust in You.

January 22
HELPING SOULS

O my Jesus, You are the life of my life. You know only too
well that I long for nothing but the glory of Your Name
and that souls come to know Your goodness. Why do souls
avoid You, Jesus?—I don't understand that. (*Diary*, 57)

Reflection

It just doesn't make sense to St. Faustina. How could someone, why
would someone, avoid Jesus? She's not asking for an answer. What
she wants is to help them "come to know Your goodness." Just as we
can say Jesus' love for each of us is unique because our relationship
with Him is one of a kind, so too is how He asks us to help others
come to know Him, and love Him.

Prayer

Dear Lord, please show me how to help N. come to know You
better.

Jesus, I trust in You.

January 23
"FAUSTINA, HOW DO I . . . ?"

O my Jesus, how very easy it is to become holy; all that is needed is a bit of good will. If Jesus sees this little bit of good will in the soul, He hurries to give himself to the soul, and nothing can stop Him, neither shortcomings nor falls—absolutely nothing. Jesus is anxious to help that soul, and if it is faithful to this grace from God, it can very soon attain the highest holiness possible for a creature here on earth. God is very generous and does not deny His grace to anyone. Indeed, He gives more than what we ask of Him. Faithfulness to the inspirations of the Holy Spirit—that is the shortest route. (*Diary*, 291)

Reflection

In the past it was asking a local resident for directions, then picking road maps, and now relying on GPS devices or smartphone apps. All with the same goal in mind; to most quickly and easily get from here to where I want to be. Today's quote is as if we asked a smart speaker: "Faustina, how do I get to holiness?" Her one-sentence answer? "Be faithful to those nudges from the Holy Spirit."

Prayer

Thank you, Faustina. I have more questions for you, but for now I'm going to spend some time thinking about today's answer.

Jesus, I trust in You.

January 24

UNFAILING STRENGTH

As I was praying to the living Heart of Jesus in the Blessed Sacrament for the intention of a certain priest, Jesus suddenly gave me knowledge of His goodness and said to me, **I will give him nothing that is beyond his strength.** (*Diary*, 1607)

Reflection

Today St. Faustina's words echo a prayer by St. Francis de Sales (1567–1622): "Do not look forward to what may happen tomorrow; the same everlasting Father who cares for you today will take care of you tomorrow and every day. Either He will shield you from suffering, or He will give you unfailing strength to bear it."

Prayer

Today, Lord, give me courage for tomorrow. And faith.

Jesus, I trust in You.

January 25
THREE DEGREES

[My confessor, Father Sopocko, said to me:] There are three degrees in the accomplishment of God's will: in the first, the soul carries out all rules and statutes pertaining to external observance; in the second degree, the soul accepts interior inspirations and carries them out faithfully; in the third degree, the soul, abandoned to the will of God, allows Him to dispose of it freely, and God does with it as He pleases, and it is a docile tool in His hands. (*Diary*, 444)

Reflection

No wonder St. Faustina put great trust in her confessor. He does such a good job — in a simple way — of describing the degrees or states of following God's will. We follow the rules. We're attuned to what He's asking us to do. And we're so head-over-heels in love with Him we say, "Whatever You want. Really. Whatever." Yes, we have room for growth but that shouldn't discourage us. God knows we have potential, and the ability to move forward.

Prayer

I want to get better at knowing, and at being more aware of, Your will for me, Lord. And then doing it, with a cheerful spirit.

Jesus, I trust in You.

January 26

THE THIN LINE

The Lord gave me to know who it is that upholds the existence of mankind: it is the chosen souls. When the number of the chosen ones is complete, the world will cease to exist. (*Diary*, 926)

Reflection

The "thin blue line" is sometimes used as a term for the police force. For the officers who safeguard us and maintain civil order. Today St. Faustina writes about another "thin line." This one is the "chosen souls," those who have been called to the priesthood and religious life. In some ways—of which she was aware because of her mystical experiences—they "uphold the existence of all mankind" and the world itself.

Prayer

The harvest is plentiful, but the laborers are few (Mt 9:37).

Lord, please send laborers into the harvest.

Jesus, I trust in You.

January 27

PRIESTS NEED OUR PRAYERS

> I have offered this day for priests. (*Diary*, 823)

Reflection

In his first address as pope, Francis asked the crowd to join him in praying for Pope Benedict XVI. Then, he continued: "And now I would like to give the blessing, but first I want to ask you a favor. Before the bishop blesses the people, I ask that you would pray to the Lord to bless me — the prayer of the people for their Bishop. Let us say this prayer — your prayer for me — in silence." All priests, from aging Pontiff to the young man most recently ordained, need our prayers. Need *your* prayers.

Prayer

Eternal High Priest, I offer this day for priests.

Jesus, I trust in You.

January 28
IN THE MIDDLE OF THE NIGHT

As often as I shall awake at night, I shall steep myself
in a prayer of thanksgiving. (*Diary*, 1367)

Reflection

St. Faustina uses a strong image in today's quote. She's not talking
about a quick word of thanks to God but "steeping" herself in a
prayer—or maybe many prayers—of thanksgiving. That deliberate "sense of gratitude" is one advocated by secular counselors as
well. It helps, especially during those dark nights, to shed the light
of truth on a situation. We see more clearly. And, spiritually, it
reminds us we're not alone. Not in the night. Not in our lives.

Prayer

Lord, hear my prayers of thanksgiving … in the middle of the night
and all through the day.

Jesus, I trust in You.

January 29
"A NOBLE AND DELICATE SOUL"

A noble and delicate soul, even the simplest, but one of delicate sensibilities, sees God in everything, finds Him everywhere, and knows how to find Him in even the most hidden things. It finds all things important; it highly appreciates all things; it thanks God for all things; it draws profit for the soul from all things; and it gives all glory to God. It places its trust in God and is not confused when the time of ordeals comes. It knows that God is always the best of Fathers and makes little of human opinion. It follows faithfully the faintest breath of the Holy Spirit; it rejoices in this Spiritual Guest and holds on to Him as a child holds on to his mother. Where other souls come to a standstill and fear, this soul passes on without fear or difficulty. (*Diary*, 148)

Reflection

Today's quote is a good checklist for us. It's worthwhile to slowly read through it again. And even to write it out as a list. What can we do today, this week, this month, to grow closer to becoming that "noble and delicate soul" St. Faustina describes? The soul God wants us to be.

Prayer

Thank you, St. Faustina, for all your good advice. For all the ways to help me draw closer to God.

Jesus, I trust in You.

January 30
ENDLESS DAYS OF VICTORY

After a while, Jesus said to me, **Paint an image [of Divine Mercy] according to the pattern you see, with the signature: Jesus, I trust in You.... I promise that the soul that will venerate this image will not perish. I also promise victory over [its] enemies already here on earth, especially at the hour of death. I Myself will defend it as My own glory.** (*Diary*, 47–48)

Reflection

An image ... and a prayer. Five short words. An act of faith that can be the basis for more deliberately living what the prayer encourages me, invites me, to do.

Prayer

Dear Jesus, Divine Mercy, help me trust You today, through all the days of my life, and at the hour of my death.

Jesus, I trust in you.

January 31
LOVED ... SPEECHLESS

What a delight it is to love with all the force of one's
soul and to be loved even more in return, to feel and
experience this with the full consciousness of one's being.
There are no words to express this. (*Diary*, 1523)

Reflection

Thunderstruck. Dumbfounded. A jaw-dropping speechlessness. As
St. Faustina says, "There are no words to express this." "This" being
the realization that no matter how completely she loved God, He
loved her "even more in return." The same is true for us. No matter
how much we may love someone, no matter how much we may
love God, His love for them and for us is ... infinitely! ... greater.
And personal. One-on-one.

Prayer

Thank You, Dear Lord, for Your infinite and eternal love for me.
Jesus, I trust in You.

CHAPTER TWO

Reflections

FOR

February

February 1

A ROAD AND A PATH

One day, I saw two roads. One was broad, covered with ...
flowers, full of joy, music and all sorts of pleasures. People ...
reached the end without realizing it. And at the end ... was
a horrible precipice; that is, the abyss of hell. The souls fell
blindly into it; as they walked, so they fell.... And I saw the
other road, or rather, a path, for it was narrow and strewn with
thorns and rocks; and the people who walked along it had tears
in their eyes, and all kinds of suffering befell them.... At the
end of the road there was a magnificent garden filled with all
sorts of happiness, and all these souls entered there. At the
very first instant they forgot all their sufferings. (*Diary*, 153)

Reflection

It's a common expression that the road to hell is paved with good
intentions but, St. Faustina is saying, it's also lined with "all sorts
of pleasures" rooted in sin and selfishness. What of the hard and
treacherous "path" to heaven? St. Faustina knew, as we know, we
don't travel it alone. Our God is always with us.

Prayer

All you saints in heaven, all you souls in purgatory, lead me home.
Jesus, I trust in You.

February 2
POVERTY, CHASTITY, AND OBEDIENCE

The Virtue of Poverty: This is an evangelical virtue which impels the heart to detach itself from temporal things; the religious, in virtue of his profession is strictly obliged to it.

The Virtue of Chastity: ... [T]here are also five means of preserving this virtue: humility, the spirit of prayer, modesty of the eyes, fidelity to the rule, a sincere devotion to the Blessed Virgin Mary.

The Virtue of Obedience: The virtue of obedience goes further than the vow; it embraces the rules, the regulations and even the counsels of the superiors. (*Diary*, 93)

Reflection

A virtue is a virtue is a virtue but one size doesn't fit all. St. Faustina is describing their roles for a religious but, with only a little thought and prayer, we can see how they apply to laity, too. How they apply to you and your life.

Prayer

Dear Lord, help me — in the state of life to which You've called me — live my own vows of poverty, chastity, and obedience.

Jesus, I trust in You.

February 3

MISERY AND MERCY

O Jesus, I have been feeling extraordinarily well, close to Your Heart, during this retreat. Nothing disturbs the depths of my peace. With one eye I gaze on the abyss of my misery and with the other, on the abyss of Your mercy. (*Diary*, 1345)

Reflection

St. Faustina has quite a view. What appears to be two bottomless pits. The first, all the troubles, complications, and pains of life on earth. The second, God's mercy. But, of course, the first is limited. All of us are "merely" passing through our time on earth, heading toward God's infinite mercy. We cannot sin enough, betray God enough, or turn our back on Him enough to deplete His mercy. Always, throughout our time here, we can repent, we can return to Him, we can again find our own deep peace in His love.

Prayer

Infinite Love, Infinite Compassion, Infinite Mercy, Infinite God, thank You.

Jesus, I trust in You.

February 4

THE THERMOMETER OF SUFFERING

True love is measured by the thermometer of suffering. Jesus, I thank You for the little daily crosses,... for poor health and loss of strength, for self-denial, for our dying to myself, for lack of recognition in everything, for the upsetting of all my plans. Thank You, Jesus, for interior sufferings, for dryness of spirit, for terrors, fears and incertitudes, for the darkness and the deep interior night ... (*Diary*, 343)

Reflection

How does a married couple forge such an incredible bond of love? Not just by going through those good times and bad, through sickness and health, but by going through them *together*. With and for each other. As one. They prove a love that can be "measured by the thermometer of suffering." Jesus' Passion and death proved His love for us. Now we have opportunities to prove ours for Him by accepting life's sufferings and heartaches and offering them up as prayers for others. Now, like that husband and wife, we can choose to go through them *as one* with Christ.

Prayer

Lord, I know suffering is never good in itself, but what it can produce—with You—is amazing.

Jesus, I trust in You.

February 5
TAKE YOUR MEDICINE!

It occurred to me to take my medicine, not by the spoonful, but just a little at a time, because it was expensive. Instantly, I heard a voice, **My daughter, I do not like such conduct. Accept with gratitude everything I give you through the superiors, and in this way you will please Me more.** (*Diary*, 1381)

Reflection

Such tenderness, concern ... and firmness. A little reprimand of St. Faustina for not taking care of herself, even if her reason was self-less. In the same way, Jesus wants us to take care of ourselves. Yes, acts of self-sacrifice to help others but not at the risk of our own health.

Prayer

O Holy Spirit, never let me confuse spiritual wisdom with temporal foolishness. Don't let me get so caught up in making personal sacrifices that they put my health at risk.

Jesus, I trust in You.

February 6

> I fervently beg the Lord to strengthen my faith, so that
> in my drab, everyday life I will not be guided by human
> dispositions, but by those of the spirit. Oh, how everything
> drags man towards the earth! But lively faith maintains the
> soul in the higher regions and assigns self-love its proper
> place; that is to say, the lowest one. (*Diary*, 210)

Reflection

As Our Lord did with Peter, James, and John, at the Transfigura-
tion, He invited St. Faustina to have a glimpse of who He really is
and what's to come. And like those three, she had to "come down
from the mountain." In a smaller way, there are times and moments
when our souls soar in prayer and grace, and after them we too need
stronger faith for our everyday lives.

Prayer

Thank You, Dear Lord, for quiet times in my everyday life. Help
me appreciate how simple and soothing they can be. Today, I will
especially pray for those who are dealing with accidents, illnesses,
or other devasting news. With hard and hectic times.

Jesus, I trust in You.

February 7

OUR SPECIAL KIND OF LOVE

I want to love You as no human soul has ever loved You before; and although I am utterly miserable and small, I have, nevertheless, cast the anchor of my trust deep down into the abyss of Your mercy, O my God and Creator! In spite of my great misery I fear nothing, but hope to sing You a hymn of glory forever. (*Diary*, 283)

Reflection

The love you and God share is like no other because *you* are like no other. Unique in all creation. For all time. If Jesus came down from heaven, took you by the hands, looked deeply into your eyes and said, "You're special," He would mean it. Trust Him. He *is* the truth.

Prayer

What a wonderful thought, Dear Lord. What a wonderful fact. No human soul has ever loved You the way I do. Help me love You more.

Jesus, I trust in You.

February 8

ALL OR NOTHING

I do not understand how it is possible not to trust in Him who can do all things. With Him, everything; without Him, nothing. He is Lord. He will not allow those who have placed all their trust in Him to be put to shame. (*Diary*, 358)

Reflection

St. Faustina is saying the opposite of what many ask today. For them, it's how can you possibly believe in God, in any god, because that's so illogical. So childish. Her question: How can you *not* believe in Him? With Him everything ... that matters. Without Him ... nothing. What a blessing, what a gift, what a grace faith is!

Prayer

Today, Dear Lord, I pray for those I know who don't know You. That's such a hard way to live. Help me — by my love for them — reflect Your love for them.

Jesus, I trust in You.

February 9

THE SILENT SOUL

The silent soul is capable of attaining the closest union with God.
It lives almost always under the inspiration of the Holy Spirit.
God works in a silent soul without hindrance. (*Diary*, 477)

Reflection

We live in a time when people of all ages have become more and
more dependent on noise. Radios, televisions, computers, elec-
tronic devices, cell phones. St. Faustina is telling us that if we want
peace and quiet … quiet comes first. To be "silent souls" we have
to, for a time, be "silent human beings." To stop and listen. Stop
the noise and distractions. And listen to—pay attention to—what
our heart wants to say to God and what, in our hearts, He's saying
to us.

Prayer

Quiet me, Lord. Calm me down. I want to better listen to You.

Jesus, I trust in You.

February 10
ASKING FOR HIS HELP

Oh, how good it is to call on Jesus for help during a conversation. Oh, how good it is, during a moment of peace, to beg for actual graces. I fear most of all this sort of confidential conversation; there is need of much divine light at times like this, in order to speak with profit, both for the other person's soul, and for one's own as well. God, however, comes to our aid; but we have to ask Him for it. (*Diary*, 1495)

Reflection

St. Faustina prays a silent and sincere, "Help me!" which the Holy Spirit answers with wisdom. What a wonderful thing to realize: God can and will help us when we're visiting with a friend who has problems and we find ourselves at a loss for words. Yes, He will come to our aid, "but we have to ask Him for it."

Prayer

Holy Spirit, give me the wisdom to know what to say, and to know when to be still.

Jesus, I trust in You.

February 11

THE FACE OF JESUS

> I steeped myself in prayer, especially for the sick. I now see how much the sick have need of prayer. (*Diary*, 826)

Reflection

In 1992 St. John Paul II instituted the World Day of the Sick to be marked on February 11, the Feast of Our Lady of Lourdes. It was to be, he wrote, "a special time of prayer and sharing, of offering one's suffering for the good of the Church and of reminding everyone to see in his sick brother or sister the face of Christ who, by suffering, dying and rising, achieved the salvation of mankind."

Prayer

Beloved Lady of Lourdes, be with those who are suffering and those who are dying. Help us, your children, to be with them — in prayer or in person — too.

Jesus, I trust in You.

February 12

"THE ABYSS OF MY MERCY"

[Jesus said to St. Faustina:] **Pray as much as you can for the dying. By your entreaties, obtain for them trust in My mercy, because they have most need of trust, and have it the least.... You know the whole abyss of My mercy, so draw upon it for yourself and especially for poor sinners. Sooner would heaven and earth turn into nothingness than would My mercy not embrace a trusting soul.** (*Diary*, 1777)

Reflection

Praying for the dying and the abyss of God's mercy are themes repeated throughout the *Diary*. Obviously, each was important to Our Lord and to St. Faustina. They were topics He wanted her to know about, think about, pray about. And, likewise, she wants us to do the same. To know, to think, to pray. To play a role in changing ... eternal ... lives.

Prayer

Dear Lord, my heart is heavy when I think of N. Help them open their heart to You.

Jesus, I trust in You.

February 13

THE CHAPLET FOR THE DYING

... [T]he Lord said to me, **My daughter, help Me to save a certain dying sinner. Say the chaplet that I have taught you for him....** I understood how very important the chaplet was for the dying. (*Diary*, 1565)

Reflection

Over the years, Our Lord was educating St. Faustina so she could teach the world—could teach us—about Divine Mercy. Among the "pillars" that Jesus presented to her was the chaplet. (Along with the image, novena, and holy hour.) In today's quote Jesus tells us to pray this powerful devotion for those who are near death. It's an act, St. Faustina says, that's "very important."

Prayer

Eternal Father, I offer You the Body and Blood, Soul and Divinity of Your dearly beloved Son, Our Lord Jesus Christ, in atonement for our sins and those of the whole world. I do this now for those who are dying.

Jesus, I trust in You.

February 14

JESUS, YOU ARE MY ...

Jesus, Friend of a lonely heart, You are my haven. You are my peace. You are my salvation, You are my serenity in moments of struggle and amidst an ocean of doubts. You are the bright ray that lights up the path of my life. You are everything to a lonely soul. You understand the soul even though it remains silent. You know our weaknesses, and like a good physician, You comfort and heal, sparing us sufferings—expert that You are. (*Diary*, 247)

Reflection

Today's quote reads like a litany because it is. There's a repetition to it. A rhythm. A drawing us into a prayerful frame of mind. It isn't just saints and popes, clerics and religious, who can write litanies. We can, too. If we close our eyes and open our hearts and whisper what's in our soul.

Prayer

Jesus, You are my ... Jesus, You are my ... Jesus, You are my ...
Jesus, I trust in You.

February 15

LET IT BE

I understand souls who are suffering against hope, for I have gone through that fire myself. But God will not give [us anything] beyond our strength. Often have I lived hoping against hope, and have advanced my hope to complete trust in God. Let that which He has ordained from all ages happen to me. (*Diary*, 386)

Reflection

At times time we all feel hopeless and St. Faustina was no exception. In her words, she had "gone through that fire myself." And what did it teach her? Trust what God had planned for her since before time. Some of it wonderful. Some of it hard. Like the Blessed Virgin Mary, St. Faustina said, "Let it be." That can be our choice, our prayer, too.

Prayer

Let it be done unto me according to Your will, Dear Lord.

Jesus, I trust in you.

February 16

PRISONS AND CONVENTS

O my Jesus, when shall we look upon souls with higher motives in mind? When will our judgments be true? You give us occasions to practice deeds of mercy, and instead we use the occasions to pass judgment. In order to know whether the love of God flourishes in a convent, one must ask how they treat the sick, the disabled, and the infirm who are there. (*Diary*, 1269)

Reflection

St. Faustina is echoing the point made by nineteenth-century novelist Fyodor Dostoyevsky who wrote: "The degree of civilization in a society can be judged by entering its prisons." She's saying if someone wants to know if God's love is flourishing in a convent, see how they treat the sick and frail. And if we want gauge just how loving and merciful we're being? We need only compare our actions and attitudes to the Spiritual and Corporal Works of Mercy.

Prayer

Heavenly Father, through all of today, help me to be less judgmental and more merciful.

Jesus, I trust in You.

February 17
FIVE WOUNDS

> As I was praying before the Blessed Sacrament and greeting
> the five wounds of Jesus, at each salutation I felt a torrent of
> graces gushing into my soul, giving me a foretaste of heaven
> and absolute confidence in God's mercy. (*Diary*, 1337)

Reflection

Lent is an especially appropriate time to "greet"—to meditate
on—Jesus' five wounds. Traditionally, they're the feet, hands, and
side of the crucified Christ. Wounds that the Risen Jesus still bears
today. "Then he said to Thomas, 'Put your finger here, and see my
hands; and put out your hand, and place it in my side; do not be
faithless, but believing'" (Jn 20:27).

Prayer

My Lord and my God.
　　Jesus, I trust in You.

February 18

THE GREATEST MIRACLES

[Jesus said to St. Faustina:] **Write, speak of My mercy. Tell souls where they are to look for solace; that is, in the Tribunal of Mercy** [The sacrament of Reconciliation]. **There the greatest miracles take place [and] are incessantly repeated. To avail oneself of this miracle, it is not necessary to go on a great pilgrimage or to carry out some external ceremony; it suffices to come with faith to the feet of My representative and to reveal to him one's misery, and the miracle of Divine Mercy will be fully demonstrated.** (*Diary*, 1448)

Reflection

"The greatest miracles take place...." In whispered tones. With hesitation, regret, and sometimes fear. With honesty, humility, faith, and sometimes tears and relief. With forgiveness, grace, and new life. Always, new life. The greatest miracles take place through the Sacrament of Reconciliation.

Prayer

O God, I want to take better advantage of the miracle of Your mercy.

Jesus, I trust in You.

February 19
MY EXCLUSIVE TASK

Grant that I may have love, compassion and mercy for every soul without exception. O my Jesus, each of Your saints reflects one of Your virtues; I desire to reflect Your compassionate heart, full of mercy; I want to glorify it. Let Your mercy, O Jesus, be impressed upon my heart and soul like a seal, and this will be my badge in this and the future life. Glorifying Your mercy is the exclusive task of my life. (*Diary*, 1242)

Reflection

One of St. Faustina's blessings was knowing "the exclusive task of my life." How did she discover that? How was it revealed to her? With her taking one small tentative step a time. With minute after minute spent in prayer. With a gradual unfolding of God's will, God's plan, for her and her alone. Our Heavenly Father invites us to do the same. To listen and speak to Him. To take those small steps. To observe and accept the unfolding of His will in our life.

Prayer

Lead me on, Lord.

Jesus, I trust in You.

February 20

IT'S BEYOND US

My Jesus, You alone are good. Even if my heart were to make every effort to write of Your goodness, at least in part, I could not do so—this is beyond all our comprehension. (*Diary*, 1800)

Reflection

It's amazing, and silly, that we humans think we can completely know, understand, or explain God. A creature is never greater than its Creator. Still, in so many ways, we try to do just that. If God doesn't fit our (narrow) definition of who He is, then.... Our faith is shaken. Or, more drastic, we decide there is no God. At some point we have to accept what St. Faustina accepted: "this is beyond all our comprehension." And then today and every day on earth, live with that.

Prayer

All-powerful, all-knowing, all-loving, eternal God, thank You.
    Jesus, I trust in You.

February 21

A TASTE OF HEAVEN ON EARTH

No greater joy is to be found than that of loving God. Already here on earth we can taste the happiness of those in heaven by an intimate union with God, a union that is extraordinary and often quite incomprehensible to us. One can attain this very grace through simple faithfulness of soul. (*Diary*, 507)

Reflection

Every day, throughout my day, Jesus offers me the opportunities to "already here on earth, taste the happiness of those in heaven." What am I doing with them?

Prayer

Dear Father, Beloved Son, and Holy Spirit, I want to grow closer to You today. Help me do that every day until I, too, taste the happiness of heaven completely and forever.

Jesus, I trust in You.

February 22
THROUGH THE HEART OF JESUS

When I make the Way of the Cross, I am deeply moved at the twelfth station. Here I reflect on the omnipotence of God's mercy which passed through the Heart of Jesus. In this open wound of the Heart of Jesus I enclose all poor humans ... and those individuals whom I love, as often as I make the Way of the Cross. From that Fount of Mercy issued the two rays; that is, the Blood and the Water. With the immensity of their grace they flood the whole world ... (*Diary*, 1309)

Reflection

Sometimes we say "if I could see it through her eyes" or "walk a mile in his shoes." The gift Jesus gave St. Faustina was to see the world, see us, through His heart. What did it show?

Mercy. For each and every one of us. For you.

Prayer

Oh, Dear Lord, Fount of Mercy, thank You for dying for me. Thank You, despite all the ways I've turned from You, for loving me. Still. And always.

Jesus, I trust in You.

February 23
THE LITTLE-T "TRINITY" OF PRAYER

The Lord God grants His graces in two ways: by inspiration
and by enlightenment. If we ask God for a grace, He will give
it to us; but let us be willing to accept it. And in order to
accept it, self-denial is needed. Love does not consist in words
or feelings, but in deeds. It is an act of the will; it is a gift;
that is to say, a giving. The reason, the will, the heart — these
three faculties must be exercised during prayer. (*Diary*, 392)

Reflection

It's amazing what St. Faustina can pack into less than one hundred
words. That's why it's probably a good idea to slowly reread today's
quotation. Grace, acceptance, self-denial, love, deeds, gifts, and
giving. Then the little-*t* "trinity of prayer": the reason, the will, the
heart. What one point, one insight, one theological gem, can you
focus on today?

Prayer

Thank You for the saints, Dear Heavenly Father. Thank you for the
holy ones who've lived among us — and the ones who live among
us still — who share their wisdom with us. Who tell us what You
told them. Who, by words and example, lead us to You.

Jesus, I trust in You.

February 24

YOU LIKE TO BE WITH ME

The moments which are most pleasant to me are those
when I converse with the Lord within the center of
my being. I try my very best not to leave Him alone.
He likes to be always with us ... (*Diary*, 1793)

Reflection

Imagine that. Growing close enough to Jesus to realize He likes to
be with me. Always. Because He does. Always. But how do I reach
that point in our relationship? "Conversing"—talking and listening—with Him in "the center of my being." He allows it to happen. I, today and tomorrow and always, can spend time in prayer
with Him, doing my part to make it happen.

Prayer

I hear echoes of the words of St. Elizabeth, dear Jesus: "And why is
this granted me, that the mother my Lord should come to me?" (Lk
1:43). Why is this granted me? That You *like* to be with me? Thank
You for being ... You. Help me become the "me" You created me to
be.

Jesus, I trust in You.

February 25

WHEN WORDS FAIL US

O my Jesus, You Yourself must put words into my mouth,
that I may praise You worthily. (*Diary*, 1605)

Reflection

Probably most of us are tongue-tied sometimes. We're young and more than deeply smitten (and nervous!) and can't quite get out the words "I love you." We're introduced to someone famous or someone we truly admire and stand there speechless. Fortunately, God knows our minds and our hearts and so, as we stumble along, He hears our prayer without us even putting it into thoughts or words or voice. On the other hand, today is a good day to say some things to others. Things like "I love you," "Thank you," "Good job," and "I forgive you."

Prayer

Sometimes, Lord, when I'm with You before the Blessed Sacrament or home alone with You, I'm speechless. Thank You, that that's OK. Thank You for the quiet times we have together.

Jesus, I trust in You.

February 26

THE WARRIORS AMONG US

... O my Jesus, I know that, in order to be useful to souls, one has to strive for the closest possible union with You, who are Eternal Love. One word from a soul united to God effects more good in souls than eloquent discussions and sermons from an imperfect soul. (*Diary*, 1595)

Reflection

It's not uncommon for those who are elderly to ask themselves, and others, "Why am I still here?" St. Faustina—who, though young— had her own serious health problems, offers the answer. Souls closest to Our Lord are the souls most helpful for others. Though bedbound, housebound, or mentally or physically limited in so many ways, they are "prayer warriors." They are a gift, a treasure. Their prayers, including and especially the offering up of their suffering for others, are powerful blessings for all of us. Today, what can we do for one of them?

Prayer

Thank You, Dear Lord, for the prayers and examples of the suffering among us. For the times I've forgotten them. For the times I've failed to visit them, thank them, and show them my love for them. Like You—crucified—their pain, their agony, their way of the cross and death, change the world ... and me.

Jesus, I trust in You.

February 27
NOT BY HEROIC DEEDS

I strive for the greatest perfection possible in order to be useful to the Church.... I have come to understand how great an influence I have on other souls, not by any heroic deeds, as these are striking in themselves, but by small actions like a movement of the hand, a look, and many other things too numerous to mention, which have an effect on and reflect in the souls of others,... (*Diary*, 1475)

Reflection

Every hive needs worker bees. Not glamourous or heroic, just insects that, day after day, get the job done. That venture out, gather pollen, and return with it. "Saving" souls can sound both glamourous and heroic. "Touching" souls ... is what most of us are called to do. Day after day. A look of kindness. A word of support. A silent prayer.

Prayer

I want to get better at thinking small, Lord. At thinking local. At seeing those who walk among me so hungry for the look, the word, or the prayer that will transform their day. I want to do that, Lord.

Jesus, I trust in You.

February 28
WELL, I THOUGHT OF YOU *FIRST*!

When I received Holy Communion, I said to Him, "Jesus, I thought about You so many times last night," and Jesus answered me, **And I thought of you before I called you into being.** "Jesus, in what way were You thinking about me?" **In terms of admitting you to My eternal happiness.** After these words, my soul was flooded with the love of God. I could not stop marveling at how much God loves us. (*Diary*, 1292)

Reflection

Once again, St. Faustina — this Bride of Christ — sounds like a newlywed loving her groom. "I thought about You so many times"! But this time, Jesus, sounding like a newlywed loving His bride, one-ups her. He says, "I thought of you before I called you into being." Top that!

Prayer

You thought of *me* before You called me into being, Lord. I really love the feel rather than the sound of it.

Jesus, I trust in You.

February 29 (Leap Year)
"THE SEAL OF YOUR MERCY"

O my Jesus, teach me to open the bosom of mercy
and love to everyone who asks for it. Jesus, my
Commander, teach me so that all my prayers and deeds
may bear the seal of Your mercy. (*Diary*, 755)

Reflection

Jesus has a lot of titles, but "Commander" seems unique to St. Faustina. Maybe the term is a little jarring because—yes, He commands and, yes, there are the Commandments—but ... "No longer do I call you servants, for the servant does not know what his master is doing; but I have called you friends, for all that I have heard from my Father I have made known to you" (Jn 15:15). It's our Friend who can teach us about mercy and love, and about our Heavenly Father.

Prayer

Like Your mercy, Your kindness and love are overwhelming. Thank You for Your confidence in me, Dear Commander, that I can get better and better at all three.

Jesus, I trust in You.

CHAPTER THREE

Reflections

FOR

March

March 1

WHAT'S ON YOUR LIST?

O my Jesus, my Master, I unite my desires to the desires that You had on the cross: I desire to fulfill Your holy will; I desire the conversion of souls; I desire that Your mercy be adored; I desire that the triumph of the Church be hastened; I desire the Feast of Mercy to be celebrated all over the world; I desire sanctity for priests;... I desire that souls who live in our homes do not offend God, but persevere in good; I desire that the blessing of God descend upon my parents and my whole family;... (*Diary*, 1581)

Reflection

Notice that St. Faustina wants a *lot* and isn't shy about asking Jesus for it. But note, too, that the only thing she asks for herself is to do His will. All the rest of that long list is concern for the well-being of others. Today's quote raises the disturbing question: What's on my list?

Prayer

Thank You, Lord, for hearing my prayers for others. Thank You, Lord, for always taking care of me.

Jesus, I trust in You.

March 2

A "SMALL" LENT

Small practices for Lent. Although I wish and desire to do so, I cannot practice big mortifications as before,... (*Diary*, 934)

Reflection

Sometimes our own health, or the health of someone in our care, means we aren't able to have a "normal" Lent. The kind we've observed in the past, the kind that means so much to us. It can help to notice it well may be our *not* being able to fast, *not* being able to get to church as often as we'd like, *not* being able to attend the Holy Week liturgies, are huge sacrifices. Are huge prayers.

Prayer

Heavenly Father, I know You accept my Lenten sacrifices, whether big or small. I offer them all with love.

Jesus, I trust in You.

March 3

LOVE MAKES DEEDS GREAT

Jesus, You have given me to know and understand in what a soul's greatness consists: not in great deeds but in great love. Love has its worth, and it confers greatness on all our deeds. Although our actions are small and ordinary in themselves, because of love they become great and powerful before God. (*Diary*, 889)

Reflection

It wasn't much, what some members of the crowd offered. A few loaves of bread. Some fish. A small sacrifice, a small deed. Given with love. And what a difference that made. What we say and what we do can seem so tiny compared to what others have said and done. Can seem tiny to *us*. But not in the eyes of God.

Prayer

Thank You for not asking us to *do* great things, Lord, but to *love* greatly.

Jesus, I trust in You.

March 4

TOUCH ME, HEAL ME

When I receive Holy Communion, I entreat and
beg the Savior to heal my tongue, that I may
never fail in love of neighbor. (*Diary*, 590)

Reflection

Time and again the Gospels tell of crowds pushing in to get closer
to Jesus. To touch Him, or even the hem of His garment. In Holy
Communion, He comes to us. One-to-one. And, for a moment, in
the Eucharist He rests on our tongue. The same tongue that can be
used for words that praise Him and encourage others, or can spew
meanness. Our choice.

Prayer

Thank You, Dear Lord, for letting me receive You in the Eucharist.
Let all my words be those of praise to You and kindness to others.

Jesus, I trust in You.

March 5
CHATTERBOXES

My room is next to the men's ward. I didn't know that men were such chatterboxes. From morning till late at night, there is talk about various subjects. The women's ward is much quieter. It is women who are always blamed for this; but I have had occasion to be convinced that the opposite is true. It is very difficult for me to concentrate on my prayer in the midst of these jokes and this laughter. They do not disturb me when the grace of God takes complete possession of me, because then I do not know what is going on around me. (*Diary*, 803)

Reflection

It's easy to imagine St. Faustina smiling as she reveals the little secret, the little truth, she's discovered about male "chatterboxes." More seriously, she's reminding us that finding a quiet place to pray can take some effort, and that praying when there is no quiet can be even more challenging.

Prayer

Thank You, Lord, for the quiet times that we can spend together, just you and me. Help me stay close to You even when my days get busy.

Jesus, I trust in You.

March 6

MIND AND HEART, FOR THE SOUL

I will call to mind the Passion of Jesus at each confession,
to arouse my heart to contrition. (*Diary*, 225)

Reflection

Oftentimes brilliance is very simple. What if we reflected on
Christ's Passion as the first step in our examination of conscience
and then went to confession?

Prayer

Dear Lord, when I think about what You did *for* me and what I do
to you.... Dear Lord, I'm so, so sorry.

Jesus, I trust in You.

March 7

IN HIS PASSIONATE PRAYERS

> This evening, I saw the Lord Jesus just as He was during His Passion. His eyes were raised up to His Father, and He was praying for us. (*Diary*, 736)

Reflection

It's a startling image: in the midst of His Passion, Jesus is praying to the Father ... for us. For you. Such was, and is, His infinite love for us. For you.

Prayer

Beloved Jesus, help me look upon the crucifix with new eyes to better see Your love for me.

Jesus, I trust in You.

March 8

REFLECTING, NOT FASTING

At the beginning of Lent, I asked my confessor for some mortification for this time of fast. I was told not to cut down on my food but, while eating, to meditate on how the Lord Jesus, on the Cross, accepted vinegar and gall. This would be my mortification. I did not know that this would be so beneficial to my soul. The benefit is that I am meditating constantly on His sorrowful Passion and so, while I am eating, I am not preoccupied with what I am eating, but am reflecting on my Lord's death. (*Diary*, 618)

Reflection

A good confessor, a solid spiritual director, is a true gift from God. Alone, we may think *this* will be best for us, not seeing its pitfalls. Not seeing why *that* is much better. Just as God's will for us is unique, so too is the combination of good people with whom He fills our life to help us do that will.

Prayer

Dear Lord, I want to observe this Lent as You want me to. Help me know what that is.

Jesus, I trust in You.

March 9

POSTURES OF PRAYER

I recall that I have received most light during adoration which I made lying prostrate before the Blessed Sacrament for half an hour every day throughout Lent. During that time I came to know myself and God more profoundly. (*Diary*, 147)

Reflection

It's easy to shrug, let ourselves off the hook, when we read how St. Faustina prayed during Lent. How wonderful for her but.... But what? She was in a convent with a chapel. In our own lives, in our own homes, how can we pray daily during Lent? How can we come to know ourselves and God more profoundly? The Good Lord provides.

Prayer

Lord, help me find the time, the place, and the way to pray during this Lent.

Jesus, I trust in You.

March 10

JUST SAY NO

Now I understand well that what unites our soul most closely to God is self-denial; that is, joining our will to the will of God. This is what makes the soul truly free, contributes to profound recollection of the spirit, and makes all life's burdens light, and death sweet. (*Diary*, 462)

Reflection

When it comes to God's will, saying no to ourselves is saying yes to Him. And that, St. Faustina tells us, "makes all life's burdens light, and death sweet."

Prayer

I know what You want for me is what's best for me, Dear Heavenly Father. Help me choose that today and every day.

Jesus, I trust in You.

March 11

OUR PROMISES TO PRAY

My sister [Wanda] came to see me today. When she told me
of her plans, I was horror-stricken.... For no other soul did
I bring so many sacrifices and sufferings and prayers before
the throne of God as I did for her soul. I felt that I had
forced God to grant her grace. When I reflect on all this,
I see that it was truly a miracle. Now I can see how much
power intercessory prayer has before God. (*Diary*, 202)

Reflection

It's often the case that the older we get the more people we have
to pray for. The more we promise to pray for, and we want to keep
those promises. And the same with intentions. For this and for that.
Each important, each helped by our prayers. Still, it can be challenging to remember all of them when we are praying. How kind
God is, how understanding, that He listens when we summarize
with "and for all those people and intentions for whom I've promised to pray." That, too, has "much power ... before God."

Prayer

Dear Lord, I pray for all those for whom I've promised to pray. My
spirit is willing even when my memory is weak.

Jesus, I trust in You.

March 12
THE POWER OF PATIENCE

I have learned that the greatest power is hidden in patience.
I see that patience always leads to victory, although not
immediately; but that victory will become manifest after
many years. Patience is linked to meekness. (*Diary*, 1514)

Reflection

Who would have considered patience powerful? A nun who had
decades of practicing it among her fellow community members.
Practicing it *because* of her fellow community members. And what
was her victory? Greater meekness, that is, becoming more like her
beloved Jesus.

Prayer

Thank You for Your infinite patience with me, Dear Lord. Help me
be more patient with others … and with myself.

Jesus, I trust in You.

March 13

FATHER'S HELPER

Lent is a very special time for the work of priests. We should assist them in rescuing souls. (*Diary*, 931)

Reflection

We can be quick to volunteer at the parish: helping out as an usher, lector, extraordinary minister of the Eucharist, member of the St. Vincent de Paul Society or Legion of Mary, and so on. But we can be slow to realize we're called to play a role in "rescuing souls." How? Again, by our prayers, by our acts of kindness and mercy, and by our living our faith.

Prayer

Thank You, Dear Lord, for calling me to be a disciple to my family, my parish, my workplace, and my neighborhood.

Jesus, I trust in You.

March 14

SLIDING FROM "HOSANNA" TO "CRUCIFY HIM"

Palm Sunday.... During Mass, Jesus gave me to know the pain of His soul, and I could clearly feel how the hymns of *Hosanna* reverberated as a painful echo in His Sacred Heart. My soul, too, was inundated by a sea of bitterness, and each *Hosanna* pierced my own heart to its depths. My whole soul was drawn close to Jesus. I heard Jesus' voice: **My daughter, your compassion for Me refreshes Me. By meditating on My Passion, your soul acquires a distinct beauty.** (*Diary*, 1657)

Reflection

It's striking to look at Jesus' triumphant entry into Jerusalem from His point of view. From the one who knew what those people would be saying and doing only five short days later. Easily moving from "Hosanna" to "Crucify him." And what about us? How quickly and easily do we slide from "Jesus, I love You," to cold indifference toward others? Toward "the least" among us which, Our Lord said, means behaving that way toward Him.

Prayer

O my God, I am heartily sorry for having offended You by being indifferent to the needs of others.

Jesus, I trust in You.

March 15

THE EVENING OF HOLY THURSDAY

Holy Hour. — Thursday. During this hour of prayer, Jesus allowed me to enter the Cenacle [upper room], and I was a witness to what happened there. However, I was most deeply moved when, before the Consecration, Jesus raised His eyes to heaven and entered into a mysterious conversation with His Father. It is only in eternity that we shall really understand that moment. His eyes were like two flames; His face was radiant, white as snow; His whole personage full of majesty, His soul full of longing. At the moment of Consecration, love rested satiated — the sacrifice fully consummated.... Never in my whole life had I understood this mystery so profoundly as during that hour of adoration. Oh, how ardently I desire that the whole world would come to know this unfathomable mystery! (*Diary*, 684)

Reflection

What a blessing for St. Faustina. Like the apostles, she was an eye-witness to that first Mass in the upper room. Seeing meant believing even more, but still not fully understanding. That will come for her and us ... "in eternity."

Prayer

Body and Blood of Christ, I adore You.

Jesus, I trust in You.

March 16

SILENT JESUS

Silence is a sword in the spiritual struggle. A talkative soul will never attain sanctity. The sword of silence will cut off everything that would like to cling to the soul. We are sensitive to words and quickly want to answer back, without taking any regard as to whether it is God's will that we should speak. A silent soul is strong; no adversities will harm it if it perseveres in silence. (*Diary*, 477)

Reflection

Someone makes a smarmy remark about us or to us and we relish the clever, cutting come-back we have ready to fire back. To which St. Faustina says: Wait. Take a breath and consider Jesus' Passion, which included His torturers taking verbal shots at Him. To which He replied ... nothing.

Prayer

Dear Lord, sometimes I have a hard time biting my tongue. Forgive me for the times I've given someone a verbal smackdown.

Jesus, I trust in You.

March 17

HE SUFFERED FOR ME

Good Friday—Jesus catches up my heart into the very flame of His love. This was during the evening adoration. All of a sudden, the Divine Presence invaded me, and I forgot everything else. Jesus gave me to understand how much He had suffered for me. This lasted a very short time. An intense yearning—a longing to love God. (*Diary*, 26)

Reflection

Notice the use of the first person singular: me. How much He had suffered for *me*. For us. For you. Singular. All of that, every drop of blood, for you!

Prayer

Dear Jesus, I can never love You as much as You deserve, but please help me love You a little more today.

Jesus, I trust in You.

March 18

FROM THE CROSS, FROM THE HEART

> See what grace and reflection made out of the greatest criminal. He who is dying has much love: "Remember me when You are in paradise." Heartfelt repentance immediately transforms the soul. (*Diary*, 388)

Reflection

Just a short time before his death on a cross next to Our Lord's, the Good Thief became the Good Disciple. St. Faustina doesn't say his request came from desperation but from "grace and reflection." How would our lives change, how would our relationship with Jesus deepen, if we spent time in reflection on what He did for each of us? For you? What graces await?

Prayer

In good times and in bad, Lord, I want to be with You. Throughout this day, whatever it may hold, help me grow closer to You. Help me remember *You*, as I live now in your Kingdom on earth.

Jesus, I trust in You.

March 19

ST. JOSEPH ASKS US ...

Saint Joseph urged me to have a constant devotion to him. He himself told me to recite three prayers [the Our Father, the Hail Mary, and the Glory Be] and the *Memorare* once every day. He looked at me with great kindness and gave me to know how much he is supporting this work [of mercy]. He has promised me this special help and protection. I recite the requested prayers every day and feel his special protection. (*Diary*, 1203)

Reflection

In today's quote St. Joseph sounds like a dad, a father to us. "Listen," he says, "here's what will *really* help you. Say these three prayers." Then, as he did with St. Faustina, he looks on us with great kindness and wants us to know how much he's supporting the good that we do.

Prayer

Our Father ... Hail Mary ... Glory be ... *Memorare*.

Jesus, I trust in You.

March 20
SO HORRIBLE, SO WONDERFUL

You expired, Jesus, but the source of life gushed forth for souls, and the ocean of mercy opened up for the whole world. O Fount of Life, unfathomable Divine Mercy, envelop the whole world and empty Yourself out upon us. (*Diary*, 1319)

Reflection

Then Jesus "bowed his head and gave up his spirit" (Jn 19:30). The most horrible moment in all creation. And, the most wonderful. At that very moment "the source of life gushed forth for souls, and the ocean of mercy opened up for the whole world." The crucifixion, and our salvation.

Prayer

During this Lent, Dear Jesus, I want to spend more time meditating on what happened on Mount Calvary ... and why.

Jesus, I trust in You.

March 21

THE GRACE OF CONVERSION

[Jesus said to St. Faustina:] **When you say this prayer, with a contrite heart and with faith on behalf of some sinner, I will give him the grace of conversion. This is the prayer: "O Blood and Water, which gushed forth from the Heart of Jesus as a fount of Mercy for us, I trust in You."** (*Diary*, 186–187)

Reflection

We can't force someone into turning or returning to God. After all, God doesn't force any of us. What we can do—what Jesus is encouraging us to do—is pray for them.

Prayer

Today, Dear Lord, I pray for N.
   Jesus, I trust in You.

March 22

THE HIDEOUSNESS OF SIN

God gave me to know the whole hideousness of sin. I learned in the depths of my soul how horrible sin was, even the smallest sin, and how much it tormented the soul of Jesus. I would rather suffer a thousand hells than commit even the smallest venial sin. (*Diary*, 1016)

Reflection

There are some things we don't want to see because we can't "un-see" them. That may be the case with our sins. Yes, we admit them and properly confess them, but God doesn't reveal to us the ongoing ramifications on others because of our faults. Still, it might be good to, at times, at least consider them and realize "sin"—no matter how deeply hidden in the dark—is never completely personal. It's always communal.

Prayer

Dear Lord, sin tends to look so glamourous and attractive. Help me be better aware of how hideous it truly is.

Jesus, I trust in You.

March 23

THE LESSON IN HUMILITY

He who wants to learn true humility should reflect
upon the Passion of Jesus. (*Diary*, 267)

Reflection

Humans, created by God, know that actions speak louder than
words. The actions of our "meek and humble of heart" Savior rever-
berate through all time.

Prayer

Help me grow in meekness and humility, Dear Lord. Help me grow
closer to You, and grow more like You.

Jesus, I trust in You.

March 24

"DESIGNATED SUFFERER"

My God, although my sufferings are great and protracted, I accept them from Your hands as magnificent gifts. I accept them all, even the ones that other souls have refused to accept. You can come to me with everything, my Jesus; I will refuse You nothing. I ask You for only one thing: give me the strength to endure them and grant that they may be meritorious. Here is my whole being; do with me as You please. (*Diary*, 1795)

Reflection

In baseball terms it's the "designated hitter." The player who doesn't play a position, but instead fills in the batting order for the pitcher. St. Faustina offers to be the "designated sufferer," accepting what "other souls have refused to accept." Was that because she liked "great and protracted" suffering? Of course not. It was because she accepted "them from Your hands as magnificent gifts." As opportunities for incredibly powerful prayers. All she asked was that she be able to endure them and that they be "meritorious." That they be a grace, a blessing, for others ... on earth and in purgatory.

Prayer

Today, Dear Lord, help me see my suffering in a new light. Help me transform it into a prayer for others. And please help me endure.

Jesus, I trust in You.

March 25

A CHILD OF THE CHURCH

Almost every feast of the Church gives me a deeper knowledge of God and a special grace. That is why I prepare myself for each feast and unite myself closely with the spirit of the Church. What a joy it is to be a faithful child of the Church! Oh, how much I love Holy Church and all those who live in it! I look upon them as living members of Christ, who is their Head. (*Diary*, 481)

Reflection

Converts seem to have the edge over cradle Catholics when it comes to appreciating the Church. That's not surprising. They know what it was like to live without it, and what a treasure it is to be a part of it.

Prayer

Holy Spirit, be with those who are considering becoming Catholics. Help those of us already in the Church be good examples for them.

Jesus, I trust in You.

March 26

IN THE WOUNDS OF JESUS

> In difficult moments, I must take refuge in the wounds
> of Jesus; I must seek consolation, comfort, light and
> affirmation in the wounds of Jesus. (*Diary*, 226)

Reflection

Today's quote comes from a list of resolutions St. Faustina made
for herself. What did she mean by taking "refuge in the wounds of
Jesus"? Perhaps it's focusing on those physical signs, those tangible
reminders, of His deep love for her. A love always ready to offer "consolation, comfort, light and affirmation." The love of her
Beloved. Of our Beloved.

Prayer

Oh, Dear Jesus, Your Passion and Death is the greatest love story
ever told. Thank you for loving me so deeply.

Jesus, I trust in You.

March 27

STICKS, STONES, AND WORDS

Oh, how good it is that Jesus will judge us according to our conscience and not according to people's talk and judgments. O inconceivable goodness, I see You full of goodness in the very act of judgment. (*Diary*, 1470)

Reflection

It's so hard to be the target gossip or the butt of other people's "joke." It isn't just sticks and stones that do damage. Words, and attitudes, *do* hurt. We can take comfort in the fact that God knows the truth about us. And we need to seek His mercy because … God knows the truth about us.

Prayer

Forgive me, Lord, for the times I've said and shared unkind things about others. I want to become better at "judging not."

Jesus, I trust in You.

March 28

JESUS: ONE-TO-ONE

I often felt the Passion of the Lord Jesus in my body, although this was imperceptible [to others], and I rejoiced in it because Jesus wanted it so. But this lasted for only a short time. These sufferings set my soul afire with love for God and for immortal souls. Love endures everything, love is stronger than death, love fears nothing ... (*Diary*, 46)

Reflection

It's good to realize, and remember, my relationship with Jesus is unlike anyone else's ever has been or ever will be. Today my Lord and my God wants *me* to endure, to love, and to not be afraid.

Prayer

Loving Jesus, help me endure when my life gets complicated. Help me love when acts of kindness to others seem beyond my ability. Through You, with You, and in You, I want to be fearless in living my faith.

Jesus, I trust in you.

March 29

THIS SMALL DEED OF MINE

When a reluctance and a monotony as regards my duties begins to take possession of me, I remind myself that I am in the house of the Lord, where nothing is small and where the glory of the Church and the progress of many a soul depend on this small deed of mine, accomplished in a divinized way. Therefore, there is nothing small in a religious congregation. (*Diary*, 508)

Reflection

And, in the same way "there is nothing small" in a home. In a parish. In a workplace or neighborhood. It can be comforting to realize that even among saints, there can be "a reluctance and a monotony as regards my duties." Who depend on my "small deeds"?

Prayer

Sometimes I'm more than tired, Lord. I'm weary. My life is day after day, task after task. Help me break through my own reluctance and feelings of monotony.

Jesus, I trust in You.

March 30
THE BATTLE CONTINUES

In the adversities that I experience, I remind myself that the time for doing battle has not yet come to an end. I arm myself with patience, and in this way I defeat my assailant. (*Diary*, 509)

Reflection

Sometime it's easy to feel like a young child in the backseat of a car repeatedly asking his or her parents, "Are we there yet?" But in adult life, there is no sitting back and watching the miles, the years, roll by. Time and again, there are heartaches and hardships. There are demands that try us like gold in a furnace. That help us learn patience … and love.

Prayer

Give me patience, Lord. Now! No, Lord, give me just a little more patience today to better become more patient in the days to come.

Jesus, I trust in You.

March 31

MY LOW-STOOPING LORD

Lord, my heart is filled with amazement that You, absolute Lord, in need of no one, would nevertheless stoop so low out of pure love for us. I can never help being amazed that the Lord would have such an intimate relationship with His creatures. That again is His unfathomable goodness. (*Diary*, 1523)

Reflection

St. Faustina can't help sounding stupefied when she speaks of God's stooping so low just because He loves her. And then, not just look her in the eye but be part of "such an intimate relationship with His creatures." It's not hard to imagine the image of a grownup dropping down on one knee to face a toddler on his or her own level. God does that for us. For each of us.

Prayer

Thank You, Lord, for stooping down to my level, taking my hand, and safely walking me home with You.

Jesus, I trust in You.

CHAPTER FOUR

Reflections

FOR

April

April 1
CHRIST'S "EASTER GIFT"

Easter. During Mass, I thanked the Lord Jesus for having deigned to redeem us and for having given us that greatest of all gifts; namely, His love in Holy Communion; that is, His very own Self. At that moment, I was drawn into the bosom of the Most Holy Trinity, and I was immersed in the love of the Father, the Son and the Holy Spirit. These moments are hard to describe. (*Diary*, 1670)

Reflection

How does Jesus love us? When St. Faustina counts the ways, "Holy Communion, that is, His very own Self," tops the list as "the greatest of all gifts." A gift He continues to offer to us.

Prayer

Thank You for redeeming me, Dear Christ. Thank You, Risen Lord, for offering me Yourself in the Eucharist.

Jesus, I trust in You.

April 2

OCEAN OF MERCY

> Oh, who will comprehend Your love and Your
> unfathomable mercy toward us! (*Diary*, 80)

Reflection

"Unfathomable" was a word St. Faustina used often. She had to, describing Our Lord and the mercy He offers us. Yes, in nautical terms, it means we can't reach the bottom of it. Which is true. And, in general terms, it means it can't be fully explored or understood. We get it: God's love and mercy. That is, receive it. But we don't get it: God's love and mercy. That is, understand it. It's within us and beyond us. Seeing is believing but, when it comes to God, believing is seeing.

Prayer

Dear Holy Spirit, thank You for the gift of faith. Today I pray especially for my family members and friends and enemies who struggle to know You and for those who don't believe You exist. I want to be a good example for them of what it means to know, love, and serve You.

Jesus, I trust in You.

April 3

GOD'S GREATEST ATTRIBUTE

... I understood that the greatest attribute is love and mercy.
It unites the creature with the Creator. This immense love
and abyss of mercy are made known in the Incarnation of the
Word and in the Redemption [of humanity], and it is here that
I saw this as the greatest of all God's attributes. (*Diary*, 180)

Reflection

St. Faustina really had a way with words, choosing only two to
describe God's "greatest attribute." One says what unites us to Him.
The other, what keeps that unity intact despite what we do to harm
it. Love and mercy.

Prayer

"I believe ... by the Holy Spirit [He] was incarnate of the Virgin
Mary, and became man. For our sake he was crucified under Pontius
Pilate, he suffered death and was buried, and rose again on the third
day in accordance with the Scriptures." I believe in You, God of
love and mercy.

Jesus, I trust in You.

April 4

DIVINE MERCY SUNDAY

April 4, 1937. Low Sunday; that is, the Feast of Mercy. [The Sunday after Easter.] ... [A]fter Holy Communion my soul ... was flooded with joy beyond understanding, and the Lord gave me to experience the whole ocean and abyss of His fathomless mercy. Oh, if only souls would want to understand how much God loves them! All comparisons, even if they were the most tender and the most vehement, are but a mere shadow when set against the reality. (*Diary*, 1073)

Reflection

It's an amazing thing to read of St. Faustina's experience on what we now know as Divine Mercy Sunday. Her description is one she used often: "the whole ocean and abyss of His fathomless mercy." If only souls—that is, if only *we*—would want to understand how much God loves us!

Prayer

Divine Mercy, I know I can't truly understand Your love, but help me grasp it more and live my life accordingly.

Jesus, I trust in You.

April 5

GOD'S OVERWHELMING MERCY

God's floodgates have been opened for us. (*Diary*, 1159)

Reflection

Hang on to your hat, here comes mercy. If we want it, if we accept it, if we let it wash over us and transform who we are and how we live. Yes, the floodgates are open but, no, it's our choice. Always, always, always.

Prayer

Divine Mercy, I choose You. Thank You for choosing me.

Jesus, I trust in You.

April 6

SATAN HATES MERCY

> I have now learned that Satan hates mercy more than anything else. It is his greatest torment. (*Diary*, 764)

Reflection

Why would Satan hate mercy more than anything else? It's God restoring our relationship with Him. Unlike fallen angels, we've been offered the gift of returning to Him, knowing that, like the father of the prodigal son, He looks for us and runs to greet us.

Prayer

Thank You, Merciful Father. Thank You.

Jesus, I trust in You.

April 7

SANCTIFYING GRACE

Oh, how beautiful is a soul with sanctifying grace! (*Diary*, 916)

Reflection

Who wouldn't want it? In the words of the *Catechism of the Catholic Church*: "Sanctifying grace is a habitual gift, a stable and supernatural disposition that perfects the soul itself to enable it to live with God, to act by his love" (2000). And how do we get that and keep it? The sacraments and prayer.

Prayer

Dear Heavenly Father, today I pray for those who have died without being in the state of grace. Have mercy on them, and on the whole world.

Jesus, I trust in You.

April 8
THE CHOICE IS OURS

Today the Lord said to me, **Daughter, ... [w]hen you approach the confessional, know this, that I Myself am waiting there for you. I am only hidden by the priest, but I Myself act in your soul. Here the misery of the soul meets the God of mercy. Tell souls that from this fount of mercy ... souls draw graces solely with the vessel of trust. If their trust is great, there is no limit to My generosity. The torrents of grace inundate humble souls. The proud remain always in poverty and misery, because My grace turns away from them to humble souls.** (*Diary*, 1602)

Reflection

The bad news/good news is that we can interfere with receiving God's mercy and love. We can constrict or enhance our reception of it. Our choice. Remain "in poverty or misery" or be "inundated" with "torrents of grace." The key factor? Pride or humility. The better choice seems obvious but it may take a little thought, a little prayer, to figure out how—today—I can be less proudful and more humble. Less pompous and more prayerful. More like Jesus, who was, and is, "meek and humble of heart."

Prayer

"God, be merciful to me a sinner!" (Lk 18:13).

Jesus, I trust in You.

April 9

THE UPS AND DOWNS OF EVANGELIZATION

Today I saw the glory of God which flows from the image. Many souls are receiving graces, although they do not speak of it openly. Even though it has met up with all sorts of vicissitudes, God is receiving glory because of it; and the efforts of Satan and of evil men are shattered and come to naught. In spite of Satan's anger, The Divine Mercy will triumph over the whole world and will be worshipped by all souls. (*Diary*, 1789)

Reflection

"Vicissitudes" is an old word, dating back to the sixteenth century, that means "ups and downs." The image of Divine Mercy, courageously reported and promoted by St. Faustina, was far from an "instant hit" in all quarters. Even so, as we now know, it continues to "triumph over the whole world." In a similar way, but most likely on a much smaller scale, what we come to learn and know about God, and appropriately share with others, is also going to be met with ups and downs. Evangelization, old or new, is never a straight path on a smooth road.

Prayer

Lord, help me lead my life so — by my actions and my words — I'm telling others about You.

Jesus, I trust in You.

April 10

SO MANY CHOICES

O mankind, why do you think so little about God being truly among us? O Lamb of God, I do not know what to admire in You first: Your gentleness, Your hidden life, the emptying of Yourself for the sake of man, or the constant miracle of Your mercy, which transforms souls and raises them up to eternal life. (*Diary*, 1584)

Reflection

In today's quote St. Faustina has what might be called a "happy problem." Jesus, which of Your traits and gifts should I admire first? But she also has a serious question: why do so many "think so little about God being truly among us"? Could part of it be that those of us who do know Him aren't very good at "magnifying the Lord" so that others can see Him more clearly?

Prayer

Emmanuel, God with Us, help me better recognize and appreciate Your presence in my life.

Jesus, I trust in You.

April 11

WHAT GOD ASKS OF US

When I talked to my spiritual director [Father Sopocko] about various things that the Lord was asking of me, I thought he would tell me that I was incapable of accomplishing all those things, and that the Lord Jesus did not use miserable souls like me for the works He wanted done. But I heard words [to the effect] that it was just such souls that God chooses most frequently to carry out His plans. (*Diary*, 436)

Reflection

Do you consider yourself, and your soul, weak and inadequate when it comes to living the faith as you want to live it? Good news! God has a job for you. A specific job, just for you. Which He has not committed to anyone else. And with Him, you can do it.

Prayer

Dear Lord, I humbly submit myself—body and soul—to do what You are asking me to do.

Give me courage, Lord, and help me remember You are always with me.

Jesus, I trust in You.

April 12

EXERCISING MERCY

[Jesus said to St. Faustina:] **I am giving you three ways of exercising mercy toward your neighbor: the first—by deed, the second—by word, the third—by prayer....** [St. Faustina answered:] O my Jesus, You Yourself must help me in everything, because You see how very little I am, and so I depend solely on Your goodness, O God. (*Diary*, 742)

Reflection

What we do, what we say, and what we pray. One, two, three, simple as can be. Except, of course, simple doesn't always mean easy. Getting better at them, getting closer to what Jesus asks of us takes a lifetime. And what better way to spend our years than doing what He asks?

Prayer

Do, say, pray. Thanks for making it simple to remember, Dear Lord. But please remind me often.

Jesus, I trust in You.

April 13
ABUNDANCE OF SPIRITUAL MERCY

[Jesus said to St. Faustina:] ... [W]rite this for the many souls who are often worried because they do not have the material means with which to carry out an act of mercy. Yet spiritual mercy, which requires neither permission nor storehouses, is much more meritorious and is within the grasp of every soul. If a soul does not exercise mercy somehow or other, it will not obtain My mercy on the day of judgment. (*Diary*, 1317)

Reflection

Jesus is telling St. Faustina—and us—that the limited size of our bank account doesn't limit our ability to show mercy. (Or kindness or love.) We need only choose to do so, especially through our prayers and sacrifices. Through our interaction with others. Through our living our belief in Divine Mercy.

Prayer

Silver and gold, I have some, Lord. But what I have in abundance—Your love and mercy—I want to share with others through my prayers and sacrifices.

Jesus, I trust in You.

April 14

"HELP ME"

Today, the Lord came to me and said, **My daughter, help Me to save souls. You will go to a dying sinner, and you will continue to recite the chaplet, and in this way you will obtain for him trust in My mercy, for he is already in despair.** (*Diary*, 1797)

Reflection

Yes, the Chaplet of Divine Mercy is a powerful prayer that can help not only ourselves but others, including ones we love. And those we ... have a hard time loving. But there are two small words in today's quote that need our attention. The Lord said to St. Faustina, "Help me." He says the same to you. Today, how will you do what He asks?

Prayer

I'm honored, Dear Jesus, that You ask me to help You. And I'm a little overwhelmed. Help me pay closer attention to what, specifically, You're asking me to do. And, please, give me the grace and courage to do it.

Jesus, I trust in You.

April 15

THE ROLE OF SACRAMENTALS

... [H]oly water is indeed of great help to the dying. (*Diary*, 601)

Reflection

As you may know, holy water is a sacramental (a sacred sign, object, or action that bears some resemblance to a sacrament). In today's quote St. Faustina is telling us to use all the means at our disposal—including holy water—to help those who are dying. What would some others be? Bringing the person a scapular, rosary, holy card, and so on. In those situations we often say, "I wish there was something I could do." St. Faustina is telling us we can! Something that's a "great help."

Prayer

Dear Lord, help me do what I can for those who are dying. And for those who are losing a loved one. Grant them the grace of a happy death, which is to die in the state of grace.

Jesus, I trust in You.

April 16

LIKE A THREE-YEAR-OLD

There are times in life when the soul finds comfort only in
profound prayer. Would that souls knew how to persevere in
prayer at such times. This is very important. (*Diary*, 860)

Reflection

St. Faustina is telling us is to *repeatedly* storm heaven. To be like
a three-year-old and ask and ask and ask. Then take a breath and
ask again. "Profound" prayer is deep, sincere, personal ... and (in a
good way) unrelenting.

Prayer

When it comes to praying, Lord, I want to be a "marathoner" not a
"hundred-yard-dasher."

Jesus, I trust in You.

April 17

MORNING OFFERING

This is the day for the renewal of vows. Immediately upon my awakening, God's presence enveloped me, and I felt I was a child of God. Divine love was poured into my soul … (*Diary*, 1109)

Reflection

Yes, you may be familiar with the Morning Offering prayer and may begin your day with it. What St. Faustina says here is this: each morning, remember, and appreciate, what God is offering you.

Prayer

O Jesus, through the Immaculate Heart of Mary, thank You for what you offer me today. Help me use all of it for the greater glory of God.

Jesus, I trust in You.

April 18

"LITTLE TIME" HEROISM

O you small, everyday sacrifices, you are to me like wild flowers which I strew over the feet of my beloved Jesus. I sometimes compare these trifles to the heroic virtues and that is because their enduring nature demands heroism. (*Diary*, 208)

Reflection

One of the signs of sanctity is "heroic virtue": living faith, hope, and love, big-time. What St. Faustina is telling us is that continually making "little-time" sacrifices, also calls for heroism. Like a mother accepting a dandelion bouquet from her toddler, Jesus loves those, too.

Prayer

Today, Dear Jesus, I want to make a "bouquet" of little sacrifices for You.

Jesus, I trust in You.

April 19

EVERYTHING WANTED, EVERYTHING NEEDED

> Jesus concealed in the Host is everything to me. From the tabernacle I draw strength, power, courage and light. Here, I seek consolation in time of anguish. (*Diary*, 1037)

Reflection

What St. Faustina truly wanted, what she truly needed, she found in Jesus — "concealed" — in the Host. What could my life be like if I came before the tabernacle when I'm looking for strength, power, courage, or light? When I'm in anguish? Why am I not doing that, or not doing it more often?

Prayer

I want to spend more time with You, Eucharistic Lord. I want to make You more a part of my life and become more a part of Yours.

Jesus, I trust in You.

April 20
W.W.J.D.

Suffering is a great grace; through suffering the soul becomes like the Savior; in suffering love becomes crystallized; the greater the suffering, the purer the love. (*Diary*, 57)

Reflection

"What would Jesus do?" was a popular question in Christian circles a few years back. With W.W.J.D. popping up on bracelets, T-shirts, and bumper stickers. Today what St. Faustina isn't talking about what Jesus *would* do but what He *did* do. He suffered. It's what we do, too, but ... what do we do *with* it? Imitating Him, doing what He chose to do, we can offer up that suffering to our Heavenly Father for the good of others. And, truly, for our own good, too.

Prayer

Heavenly Father, accept my suffering of today, and this week, for the good of others. Give them comfort and strength, hope, and peace.

Jesus, I trust in You.

April 21

NOT GUILTY

The doctor did not allow me to go to the chapel to attend the Passion Service, although I had a great desire for it; however, I prayed in my own room. Suddenly I heard the bell in the next room, and I went in and rendered a service to a seriously sick person. When I returned to my room, I suddenly saw the Lord Jesus, who said, My daughter, you gave Me greater pleasure by rendering Me that service than if you had prayed for a long time. I answered, "But it was not to You, Jesus, but to that patient that I rendered this service." And the Lord answered me, Yes, My daughter, but whatever you do for your neighbor, you do for Me. (*Diary*, 1029)

Reflection

Small wonder we forget, or overlook, the fact that helping someone else is helping Jesus. The young nun feels bad she couldn't go to the chapel service and had to settle for praying in her room. Then even that was interrupted. Sometimes we can't get to church because of our own illness or the pressing needs of someone else. What does Jesus think? Well done, good and faithful servant.

Prayer

Thank You, Lord, for giving me so many ways to praise and serve You.

Jesus, I trust in You.

April 22

STARVING SOULS

For quite a long while, I felt pain in my hands, feet and side. Then I saw a certain sinner who, profiting from my sufferings, drew near to the Lord. All this for starving souls that they may not die of starvation. (*Diary*, 1468)

Reflection

Again, St. Faustina offers up her suffering (in this case a "hidden stigmata," one with no outward signs) as a prayer for others, but there's something more in today's quote. The image of those far from God who are "starving." Those, without Him, who will spiritually die. "Starving souls" are all around us and we, through our own suffering, have the opportunity (and obligation) to "feed" them.

Prayer

Jesus, You know I love You. I want to feed Your lambs and feed Your sheep.

Jesus, I trust in You.

April 23

LET OUR JUDGMENT CEASE

Oh, how great is the goodness of God, greater than we can understand. There are moments and there are mysteries of the divine mercy over which the heavens are astounded. Let our judgment of souls cease, for God's mercy upon them is extraordinary. (*Diary*, 1684)

Reflection

Perhaps we're so quick to judge others because it feels so good. If you're worse than I am, then I'm the better person. But only God knows their hearts. Only God knows how well or how poorly they've done with what He's given them and with what He's asked them to do. With what they've had to face and live with. To overcome and live without.

Prayer

Just and Merciful Judge, forgive me for my harsh judgments of others. Please, forgive me.

Jesus, I trust in You.

April 24

THE CHOICE TO BE GOOD

> Praise, O my Soul,
> the incomprehensible mercy of God.
> May all be for His glory. (*Diary*, 1590)

Reflection

Sometimes, maybe often, it's hard to understand why God is so good to us, considering how we are. How we treat others, and Him. But His "incomprehensible mercy" never stops flowing. Why? Because He loves us. Because He made us. And liked what He looked upon at the dawn of creation, He sees that it's good. *We* are good though, at times, we choose to do bad. *We* are His, always. Created in His image, today we can choose to show mercy, kindness, and love to those who treat us poorly.

Prayer

I want to praise You, Lord, with my mind and my heart, and in my soul. I thank You for the mercy You continue to show me, and I ask You to help me be merciful to others.

Jesus, I trust in You.

April 25

GOD'S TRUE CHILD

Then I heard the words, **I am glad you behaved like My true daughter. Be always merciful as I am merciful. Love everyone out of love for Me, even your greatest enemies, so that My mercy may be fully reflected in your heart.** (*Diary*, 1695)

Reflection

Now imagine hearing the words God said to St. Faustina: "You behaved like My true child." And "who I am—the Merciful One—can 'be fully reflected in your heart.'" *His* child. *Your* heart. What's getting in the way of your reflecting that mercy?

Prayer

Heavenly Father, I want to stop more often and remember I *am* "Your child." And that I have been since before all time and will be forever. Thank You so much, Father.

Jesus, I trust in You.

April 26

AN EXAMINATION OF CONSCIENCE

My daughter, in this meditation, consider the love of neighbor. Is your love for your neighbor guided by My love? Do you pray for your enemies? Do you wish well to those who have, in one way or another, caused you sorrow or offended you? Know that whatever good you do to any soul, I accept it as if you had done it to Me. (*Diary*, 1768)

Reflection

In today's quote Jesus give all of us some specific items for an examination of conscience. Love, prayer, well wishes. Doesn't sound too tough. Except, of course, it's to love as He loves. To pray for enemies. (Which certainly implies, and accepts the fact, that we all have enemies.) And to offer well wishes to those who caused us grief or offended us. And then there's the not-so-subtle reminder from Mt 25:31–46: Do for the least, doing for Jesus . . .

Prayer

Dear Lord, when I "consider the love of neighbor" I know I need to begin by asking for Your mercy. Help my love for others grow deeper and stronger. Help me live that way through concrete actions that makes a difference in their lives . . . and mine.

Jesus, I trust in You.

April 27
"BRIDGE" OF CHRIST

O Jesus, how sorry I feel for poor sinners. Jesus, grant them contrition and repentance. Remember Your own sorrowful Passion. I know Your infinite mercy and cannot bear it that a soul that has cost You so much should perish. Jesus, give me the souls of sinners; let Your mercy rest upon them.... Souls, do not be afraid of God, but trust in Him, for He is good, and His mercy is everlasting. (*Diary*, 908)

Reflection

St. Faustina—always a "Bride of Christ"—becomes a "Bridge of Christ." First, speaking to Jesus on behalf of "poor sinners" and asking Him to "remember" His own Passion and mercy. Then, speaking to "souls." Telling them not to be afraid. To "trust in Him, for He is good, and His mercy is everlasting." We can be bridges, too. Asking God to bless those for whom we're praying. And reminding those for whom we're praying that God loves them dearly. That they need not be afraid as they near death but have only to "trust in Him, for He is Good." How to remind them? Slowly, patiently, and gently.

Prayer

Beloved Good Shepherd, I pray for the ones who have strayed from You. And in particular, for those whose life on earth will end today.

Jesus, I trust in You.

April 28
DROWNED IN HIS MERCY

One day during Holy Mass, the Lord gave me a deeper knowledge of His holiness and His majesty, and at the same time I saw my own misery. This knowledge made me happy, and my soul drowned itself completely in His mercy. I felt enormously happy. (*Diary*, 1801)

Reflection

It's a powerful image. Like sliding into a soothing pool, our soul can "drown itself completely" in God's mercy. And, thanks to the sacrament of confession, that can be done so easily. But then, too, at other times — like today — I can approach Him in my private prayers, seek forgiveness, and grow deeper in knowledge of his holiness and majesty.

Prayer

Bless me, Heavenly Father, for I have sinned. O my God, I am heartily sorry especially for those sins I am too blind to see.

Jesus, I trust in You.

April 29

EYES FIXED ON THE GOSPEL

In no way do I seek perfection inquisitively, but I probe into the spirit of Jesus and fix my eyes on His deeds as summarized in the Gospel. Even if I lived a thousand years, I would not exhaust what is contained there. (*Diary*, 510)

Reflection

It's so easy to become dulled to the words and deeds given in the Gospel. We've heard them, we've read them so many times before. What if today, I looked more closely at those words and deeds to better imitate Jesus' example of service in my own life? One small parable, one small accounting. One small set of words Jesus spoke to the crowds two thousand years ago. Words He's saying to me today.

Prayer

Come, Holy Spirit, and enkindle in me a new desire, a new fire, for Your words written for me by Matthew, Mark, Luke, and John. Set my mind, my heart, and my soul ablaze.

Jesus, I trust in You.

April 30

WHO KNOWS YOU BETTER?

I understood how much God loves us, how simple He is, though incomprehensible, and how easy it is to commune with Him, despite His great majesty. With no one do I feel as free and as much at ease as with Him. Even a mother and her truly loving child do not understand each other so well as God and I do. (*Diary*, 603)

Reflection

In today's reflection St. Faustina is pointing out that no one knows us better than God does. And, despite that complete knowledge of all our sins and failings, no one loves us more. Infinite love. Infinite mercy. What would happen if we started to more deeply believe that, and act on it?

Prayer

O Lord, You've searched me and know me. When I sit, when I stand ... always and in all things. And despite my sins, my failings, and my imperfections, You love me completely. Divine Mercy, I adore You.

Jesus, I trust in You.

CHAPTER FIVE

Reflections

FOR

May

May 1

ENKINDLE IN ME

May 1, 1937. Today I felt the nearness of my Mother, my heavenly Mother, although before every Holy Communion I earnestly ask the Mother of God to help me prepare my soul for the coming of Her Son, and I clearly feel Her protection over me. I entreat Her to be so gracious as to enkindle in me the fire of God's love, such as burned in Her own pure heart at the time of the Incarnation of the Word of God. (*Diary*, 1114)

Reflection

Who better to help us prepare for Holy Communion than the one who prepared Christ for His adulthood? Who better to call upon as we prepare for a "Spiritual Communion" at home? Who better to "enkindle in us the fire of God's love" on this first day of a month dedicated to her? No one's better. It's Mary. Always Mary.

Prayer

O Mary, I crown you with "thank yous" today. Queen of the Angels, and my Queen.

Jesus, I trust in You.

May 2

A FLOWER OF THE RAREST

My particular examen is still the same; namely, union
with the merciful Christ, and silence.
The flower which I lay at the feet of the Mother of God
for May is my practice of silence. (*Diary*, 1105)

Reflection

A "particular examen" means taking a close look at a fault to be
overcome or a virtue to be strengthened. Clever—wise—St. Faustina combines two virtues (a closer union with Christ through, and
in, silence) and then takes the result to Mary as a gift. And every
Mother loves receiving a flower from her child.

Prayer

Dear Lord, help me look more closely at my virtues and grow
stronger in them. By the end of this month dedicated to Mary, I
want to have a "bouquet" ready for Your Mother.

Jesus, I trust in You.

May 3

DO IT FOR YOUR MOTHER

[Our Lady said to Faustina:] *I desire, My dearly beloved daughter,*
that you practice the three virtues that are dearest to Me—and
most pleasing to God. The first is humility, humility, and once again
humility; the second virtue, purity; the third virtue, love of God.
As My daughter, you must especially radiate with these virtues....
[St. Faustina wrote:] [M]y heart became so wonderfully
attracted to these virtues; and I practice them faithfully.
They are as though engraved in my heart. (*Diary*, 1415)

Reflection

Most of us try our best to comply when our mother says, "Do it for
me." Notice in today's quote Mary doesn't add, "After all I did for
you!" Which was a *lot*. What does she ask? Be humble. Be pure.
And love God. It's up to us to figure out the details and how to apply them in our own lives.

Prayer

Mother of Good Counsel, pray for us!
Jesus, I trust in You.

May 4

The Lord gave me an occasion to practice patience through a particular person with whom I have to carry out a certain task. She is slower than anyone I have ever seen. One has to arm oneself with great patience to listen to her tedious talk. (*Diary*, 1376)

Reflection

It's comforting to read about someone who drove a saint a little crazy. The offender means no ... offense ... but sometimes a person just rubs us the wrong way. It doesn't mean we're bad, just human. As all saints are. It means we have to work on being more patient. As all saints did.

Prayer

From slow workers and tedious talkers, Lord, deliver us! On the other hand, I should thank You for those excellent opportunities to hone my skills in being patient.

Jesus, I trust in You.

May 5

HOLY MOTHER CHURCH

O Church of God, you are the best mother, you alone can rear a soul and cause it to grow. Oh, how great is my love and respect for the Church, the best of all mothers! (*Diary*, 197)

Reflection

What a gift, what a priceless treasure, Jesus began for us. As in the times of the apostles and now, led by the Holy Spirit. Yes, over the years, members have misused it, have betrayed it, have been the source of others fleeing from it. But still, and always, it endures. Still, and always, it is one, holy, Catholic, and apostolic. It is sacramental. It is ours.

Prayer

O Dear Lord, help me be a member of Your Church who attracts others to it, who draws others closer to You.

Jesus, I trust in You.

May 6

LIFELONG LEARNING

Mary is my Instructress, who is ever teaching me how to live for God. My spirit brightens up in Your gentleness and Your humility, O Mary. (*Diary*, 620)

Reflection

Like St. Faustina did, from Mary — a teacher who's with us always — we can learn "how to live for God."

Prayer

Thank you for your patience, Dear Blessed Mother, when I'm being a wayward student.

Jesus, I trust in You.

May 7

EVERYTHING LOVE TOUCHES

> Love is a mystery that transforms everything it touches
> into things beautiful and pleasing to God. (*Diary*, 890)

Reflection

It's almost like the story of King Midas. Everything he touched turned to gold and soon it had cost him everything that mattered. But here, it's love. And everything it touches, everything we touch with it, can be transformed into something "beautiful and pleasing." Something that will outlast any gold. Something infinitely more precious.

Prayer

Today, Dear Lord, help me notice where and whom I can "touch" with love. Help me make my day and my actions something beautiful and pleasing to You.

Jesus, I trust in You.

May 8

THE FLOWER OF LOVE

Mercy is the flower of love. God is love, and mercy is His deed. In love it is conceived; in mercy it is revealed. (*Diary*, 651)

Reflection

Sometimes St. Faustina uses little words and short sentences to offer infinite truths. Love is the plant, mercy is its flower. God is love and what He does is offer mercy. When we see one we're seeing the other as well because they're inseparable. No love, no mercy. No mercy, no love. Created in His image, when we love others, we too are called to be merciful.

Prayer

Thank You, Dear Lord, for having mercy on the whole world. Thank You for having mercy on me.

Jesus, I trust in You.

May 9

THROUGH MARY

Through Her, as through a pure crystal,
Your mercy was passed on to us.
Through Her, man became pleasing to God;
Through Her, streams of grace flowed down upon us. (*Diary*, 1746)

Reflection

Through Mary ... who has been with us throughout our lives.
Through Mary ... who is with us now, leading us to her Son.
Through Mary ... who will be with us at the hour of our death and
for all eternity.

Prayer

Who am I that you, the Mother of my Lord, should come to me?
Jesus, I trust in You.

May 10

O inexhaustible treasure of purity of intention which makes all our actions perfect and so pleasing to God! (*Diary*, 66)

Reflection

Today's quote is one more example of how Jesus' yoke *is* easy and His burden *is* light (see Mt 11:28–30). What He asks of us is the "purity of our intention." That means the root reason we're trying to do something. To use the abbreviation of the Jesuits' motto, it's A.M.D.G. *Ad maiorem Dei gloriam*. To the greater glory of God.

Prayer

Thank You, Dear Lord, for not holding us accountable for the success of our endeavors. Thank You for focusing on *why* we're doing what we're doing.

Jesus, I trust in You.

May 11

ST. FAUSTINA'S "PRAYER FOR PRIESTS"

> Lord, give us holy priests; You yourself maintain them in
> holiness. O Divine and Great High Priest, may the power
> of Your mercy accompany them everywhere and protect
> them from the devil's traps and snares which are continually
> being set for the souls of priests. (*Diary*, 1052)

Reflection

What a wonderful, wonderful gift St. Faustina gives us today! A
simple, beautiful, and powerful prayer for all priests.

Prayer

[See above. We can't do better than that!]

May 12

GO AND TEACH

Feast of the Ascension. Today I accompanied the Lord Jesus as He ascended into heaven. It was about noon. I was overcome by a great longing for God. It is a strange thing, the more I felt God's presence, the more ardently I desired Him. Then I saw myself in the midst of a huge crowd of disciples and apostles, together with the Mother of God. Jesus was telling them to ... **Go out into the whole world and teach in My name.** He stretched out His hands and blessed them and disappeared in a cloud. (*Diary*, 1710)

Reflection

We like to think "Go and teach" was a message only for the apostles. But we know better. In our own time, in our own life, in our own way, we're to do the same. To go and to teach in His name.

Prayer

Help me come closer to You, Lord, so I can do a better job of helping others get closer, too.

Jesus, I trust in You.

May 13

"OUR LADY THE GUIDE"

O Mary, my dearest Mother, guide my spiritual life in such a way that it will please Your Son. (*Diary*, 240)

Reflection

Mary has so many titles, each a facet reflecting her relationship with God and with us. Each magnifying the Lord. Today St. Faustina talks about "Our Lady the Guide," the one who can help us better see our own path and stay on it. More than a compass or map, she walks with us, if we accept her offer.

Prayer

O Most Gracious Virgin Mary, to thee I come, before thee I stand, asking you to lead me, to walk with me, on my journey home.

Jesus, I trust in You.

May 14

"CHOSEN SOULS"

Today, the Lord gave me knowledge of His anger toward mankind which deserves to have its days shortened because of its sins. But I learned that the world's existence is maintained by chosen souls; that is, the religious orders. Woe to the world when there will be a lack of religious orders! (*Diary*, 1434)

Reflection

St. Faustina uses the term "chosen souls" in several places in her *Diary*. As she explains in today's quote, she's referring to members of religious orders. Part of their vocation — using an old expression — is to "storm heaven" for all of us. Part of ours, is to keep them in our prayers.

Prayer

Thank You, Dear Lord, for those who have answered Your invitation to enter religious life. Shower them with grace and blessing today and always.

Jesus, I trust in You.

May 15

MOTHER AND TEACHER

... I have experienced an increasing devotion to the
Mother of God. She has taught me how to love God
interiorly and also how to carry out His holy will in all
things. O Mary, You are joy, because through You God
descended to earth [and] into my heart. (*Diary*, 40)

Reflection

Dearest Mary. *Mater et Magistra*, Mother and Teacher. Helping
us grow in wisdom and age and grace (see Lk 2:51–52). What are
her topics for us? How to love God in our heart, mind, and soul;
and how to do what He's called us to do. What's her lesson plan?
Always individualized. Always the perfect instruction custom-fit
just for you.

Prayer

Teach me, Mary! Teach me about your dear Son.

Jesus, I trust in You.

May 16

A SOUL FREED

The love of God makes a soul free.... She knows that
she is not alone—God is her strength. (*Diary*, 890)

Reflection

What's a "freed" soul? One not snared in sin and evil. In selfishness and pride. One that knows "she" isn't in this alone during this
time on earth. One who relies on, and is never disappointed in,
the "strength" God offers her, especially through the Eucharist and
sacrament of confession.

Prayer

By Your cross and resurrection, You have set me free, Dear Jesus.
You have set me free.

Jesus, I trust in You.

May 17

GOD NEVER ABANDONS US

In times of interior desolation I do not lose my peace, because I know that God never abandons a soul, except perhaps only when the soul itself breaks the bond of love by its unfaithfulness. However, all creatures without exception depend on the Lord and are maintained by His omnipotence. Some are under the rule of love, others under the rule of justice. It depends on us under which rule we want to live, because no one is refused the aid of sufficient grace. (*Diary*, 1315)

Reflection

"Interior desolation." Now there's a powerful description, that fits our own feelings so well. Not that we always feel that way, but we all feel that way sometimes. That's when we need to remember God, who is everywhere, is there, too. Not beside us but *inside* us, calling us to live "the rule of love."

Prayer

Give me sufficient grace for today, Lord.

Jesus, I trust in You.

May 18

A CROWN OF CROWNS

I saw that God himself seemed to be opposing [my confessor], and I asked the Lord why He was acting in this way toward him, as though He were placing obstacles in the way of his doing what He himself had asked him to do. And the Lord said, **I am acting thus with him to give testimony that this work is Mine. Tell him not to fear anything; My gaze is on him day and night. There will be as many crowns to form his crown as there will be souls saved by this work.**

It is not for the success of a work, but for the suffering that I give reward. (*Diary*, 90)

Reflection

It seems the King of Kings offers each of us a Crown of Crowns. It's the "obstacles" we have to deal with, and overcome, in doing God's will that come to form our heavenly crown.

Prayer

Crown my life with many crowns—with many obstacles—Dear Lord, if that's the path You've chosen for my journey home to You.

Jesus, I trust in You.

May 19

SLOWLY, LOVINGLY

Once, when my confessor told me to say "Glory be to the Father" as my penance, it took me a very long time; and I began many times, but did not finish, because my spirit became united with God, and I could not stick to the prayer. Quite frequently, I am unwittingly enveloped by God's omnipotence and become entirely plunged in Him through love,... (*Diary*, 577)

Reflection

Today's quote from St. Faustina isn't about getting distracted as we pray, but moving deeper into that time of prayer. For us, as for her, a prayer we've said countless times over many years can be a springboard to something more profound, something more personal, something more prayerful. We, too—in our own unique way—can be "unwittingly enveloped by God's omnipotence and become entirely plunged in Him through love." How? If, every day, every prayer we say comes from our heart.

Prayer

Glory be to *You*, Heavenly Father, and to *You*, His Beloved Son. Glory be to *You*, Holy Spirit. All praise and glory to *You*, Most Holy Trinity.

Jesus, I trust in You.

May 20
LISTEN AND LEARN

The tongue is a small member, but it does big things.... God does not give Himself to a chattering soul which, like a drone in a beehive, buzzes around but gathers no honey.... A soul that has never tasted the sweetness of inner silence is a restless spirit which disturbs the silence of others. (*Diary*, 118)

Reflection

St. Faustina was a strong advocate of talk less/listen more. Her soul had "tasted the sweetness of inner silence" and she was hooked. She craved that silence shared with her Beloved Jesus. The same Jesus is waiting—silently—to spend time with you.

Prayer

Calm and silence my chattering soul, Dear Lord. I want to spend quiet time with You.

Jesus, I trust in You.

May 21

PRAYING FOR CONFESSORS

... I came to understand one thing: that I must pray
much for each of my confessors, that he might obtain
the light of the Holy Spirit, ... (*Diary*, 647)

Reflection

How many of us have done what St. Faustina decided to do? How
often have we done that? What an easy thing to do. What a wonderful, thoughtful, and powerful gift.

Prayer

Holy Spirit, I pray for all confessors, and especially for N.

Jesus, I trust in You.

May 22

"REJOICE AND BE HAPPY"

When I went out into the garden, I saw how everything was breathing the joy of spring. The trees, adorned with flowers, gave off an intoxicating odor. Everything was throbbing with joy, and the birds were singing and chirping their adoration of God and said to me, "Rejoice and be happy, Sister Faustina." (*Diary*, 1120)

Reflection

What a lovely image. St. Faustina's own little Garden of Eden. Notice she didn't overlook it. It was a place and a time for her to "rejoice and be happy." God gives us those, too. Little breaks when His will for us is to simply, and for a time deeply, rejoice and be happy. It's up to us to notice and appreciate them.

Prayer

Thank You for creating rejoicing and happiness, Dear Lord. It's some of your best work!

Jesus, I trust in You.

May 23

BE NOT AFRAID ... OF GOD

One day, when I was preparing for Holy Communion and noticed that I had nothing to offer Him, I fell at His feet, calling down all His mercy upon my poor soul: "May Your grace, which flows down upon me from Your Compassionate Heart, strengthen me for the struggle and sufferings, that I may remain faithful to You. And, although I am such misery, I do not fear You, because I know Your mercy well. Nothing will frighten me away from You, O God, because everything is so much less than what I know [Your mercy to be]—I see that clearly." (*Diary*, 1803)

Reflection

Most of us have experienced what it's like to have a stern teacher or an unforgiving boss. We keep our head down and our mouth shut, fearing that one look, one word, can land us in a world of hurt. Today St. Faustina says the opposite is true with God. Our missteps, our sins, can never eclipse the rays of Divine Mercy. And Jesus' "Compassionate Heart" will strengthen us for *our* "struggle and sufferings." Today we can take comfort knowing Divine Mercy is our Prince of Peace.

Prayer

Help me calm down, Lord, when I'm overwhelmed. Help me return to You, Lord, when I stray. Let me be with You always and in all things.

Jesus, I trust in You.

May 24

THE DIVINE EXAMPLE

He who knows how to forgive prepares himself for many graces from God. As often as I look upon the cross, so often will I forgive with all my heart. (*Diary*, 390)

Reflection

St. Faustina seems to be saying that our hearts, our minds, our souls are like gardens. The plants bear more fruit, the flowers have more blossoms, the better we prepare the soil. In a similar way, forgiveness prepares us for grace. And when we're hesitant to forgive, we can imitate St. Faustina and look at, and remember, the Crucified Christ.

Prayer

Soften my heart, Dear Lord, and forgive my acts of pride. Today help me offer the forgiveness I've stubbornly resisted giving.

Jesus, I trust in You.

May 25

HOPE AND THE HOLY SPIRIT

God will not give [us anything] beyond our strength. Often have I lived hoping against hope, and have advanced my hope to complete trust in God. Let that which He has ordained from all ages happen to me. (*Diary*, 386)

Reflection

In the words of the *Catechism of the Catholic Church*: "Hope is the theological virtue by which we desire the kingdom of heaven and eternal life as our happiness, placing our trust in Christ's promises and relying not on our own strength, but on the help of the grace of the Holy Spirit" (1817).

Prayer

Today, Holy Spirit, I ask you for the grace to place my hope, and my trust, in Christ's promises. Today, Holy Spirit, let what God has "ordained from all ages happen to me."

Jesus, I trust in You.

May 26

> The Feast of the Most Holy Trinity. During Holy Mass, I
> found myself suddenly united with the Most Holy Trinity.
> I recognized His majesty and greatness. I was united to the
> Three Persons. And once I was united to One of these Most
> Venerable Persons, I was, at the same time, united to the
> other Two Persons. The joy and happiness that my soul felt
> is beyond description. It grieves me that I am unable to put
> down in words that which has no words. (*Diary*, 1129)

Reflection

There's room in the Holy Trinity for each of us. Through our love,
through our doing God's will, we're invited to join them. How is
that possible, how can it be explained? "I am unable to put down in
words that which has no words."

Prayer

Glory be to the Father, and to the Son, and to the Holy Spirit. As it
was in the beginning, is now, and ever shall be, world without end.
Amen.... Love without end. Amen.

Jesus, I trust in You.

May 27

NO ONE ON EARTH IS A+

... [D]uring adoration ... God suddenly swept over me, and I was caught up in spirit before the majesty of God. I saw how the Angels and the Saints of the Lord give glory to God. The glory of God is so great that I dare not try to describe it, because I would not be able to do so, and souls might think that what I have written ... is all there is.... Now I have seen the way in which I adore God; oh, how miserable it is! ... O my God, how good You are to accept my praise as well, and to turn Your Face to me with kindness and let us know that our prayer is pleasing to You. (*Diary*, 1604)

Reflection

St. Faustina apologizes for how poorly she describes her vision of heaven and how she prays. No, we're not perfect at it and aren't going to be. But, yes—through the grace of God—we can get better at it. Today we can remember that, as we persevere, God is turning His face to us, to you, with kindness.

Prayer

Thank you, Lord. Your kindness endures forever!

Jesus, I trust in You.

May 28

CARRYING ME

... I live in the deepest peace, because the Lord Himself is
carrying me in the hollow of His hand. (*Diary*, 1264)

Reflection

These days we would say "palm," not "hollow." It's the same word
used in a traditional Irish blessing: "And until we meet again, may
God hold you in the hollow of his hand." Irish or Polish, it's a comforting image, especially when we feel frightened or lonely. And it's
an accurate one, too.

Prayer

The hollow of Your hand, Dear Lord. There's no place I'd rather be
... now and forever.

Jesus, I trust in You.

May 29

GOD IS FLUENT IN "SILENCE"

Silence is so powerful a language that it reaches the
throne of the living God. Silence is His language,
though secret, yet living and powerful. (*Diary*, 888)

Reflection

One of the many good things about personal, private prayer is it's
never sacrilegious to say, "God, I just can't find the words." We
don't have to. He's fluent in "silence."

Prayer

Let's spend more quiet time together, Lord. Just You and I.
   Jesus, I trust in You.

May 30
A "LIVING HOST"

When I had received Jesus in Holy Communion, my heart cried out with all its might, "Jesus, transform me into another host! I want to be a living host for You. You are a great and all-powerful Lord; You can grant me this favor." ... O my Jesus, I understand the meaning of "host," the meaning of sacrifice. I desire to be before Your Majesty a living host; that is, a living sacrifice that daily burns in Your honor. (*Diary*, 1826)

Reflection

Throughout her *Diary*, St. Faustina uses the image of a host to describe what she wants to do and become. That was — in her own small ways, and through her own painful and personal experiences — to imitate the suffering and sacrifice of Christ, and to join hers to His. In our own small ways and experiences, we can choose to do the same.

Prayer

Dear Jesus, help me be more like You. Help me offer up my own heartaches and hardships for others.

Jesus, I trust in You.

May 31

OUR SOUL-FILLING GOD

God filled my soul with the interior light of a deeper
knowledge of Him as Supreme Goodness and Supreme
Beauty. I came to know how very much God loves
me. Eternal is His love for me. (*Diary*, 16)

Reflection

Every human life has its share of dark times and murky paths. But
as He did with St. Faustina, He can fill our soul with "the interior
light of a deeper knowledge of Him as Supreme Goodness and Supreme Beauty." Why? Love. How? By our cooperating with Him.

Prayer

God of goodness and beauty, fill my soul.
    Jesus, I trust in You.

CHAPTER SIX

Reflections

FOR

June

June 1

> With my heart I encompass the whole world, especially
> countries which are uncivilized or where there is persecution.
> I am praying for mercy upon them. (*Diary*, 742)

Reflection

It's easy to get locked into our own little world and over-focused
on our own (big or little) problems. It can take deliberate effort to
remember that there are people who barely have enough to survive.
That there are places where they face constant and brutal perse-
cution. These are men, women, and children who need our help,
including our prayers.

Prayer

Savior of the World, I pray for the hungry, the homeless, the perse-
cuted, and those without hope.

Jesus, I trust in You.

June 2

HUMDRUM, DARK DAYS

O humdrum days, filled with darkness, I look upon you with a solemn and festive eye. How great and solemn is the time that gives us the chance to gather merits for eternal heaven! I understand how the saints made use of it. (*Diary*, 1373)

Reflection

Today we have a saint offering advice on imitating the saints, just as she did. She recommends taking advantage of "humdrum days, filled with darkness" to "gather merits" for heaven. In other words, a really bad day can be a really good day for offering up one's hardships.

Prayer

O Dear Lord, help me use my own "humdrum days" to help others and to move closer to heaven.

Jesus, I trust in You.

June 3
LESSONS IN (AND ON) LOVE

[The Feast of] Corpus Christi. During prayer, I heard these words: **My daughter, let your heart be filled with joy. I, the Lord, am with you. Fear nothing. You are in My heart.** At that moment, I knew the great majesty of God, and I understood that nothing could be compared with one single perception of God. Outward greatness dwindles like a speck of dust before one act of a deeper knowledge of God. (*Diary*, 1133)

Reflection

Through St. Faustina's reports on her visions, we see that Jesus, the Rabbi, the teacher, repeats His lessons. And Mary—the "classroom mother"—goes over them with us later. Be a person of joy. God is always with you and loves you dearly. Don't be afraid. We're to learn them … and live them.

Prayer

How amazing it is to be Your disciple, Lord. Your student.

Jesus, I trust in You.

June 4

Thank You, O Holy Trinity, for the vastness of the graces
Which You have lavished on me unceasingly through life.
My gratitude will intensify as the eternal dawn rises,
When, for the first time, I sing to Your glory. (*Diary*, 1286)

Reflection

The vastness of the graces of the Holy Trinity stretch far beyond sea to sea or age to age. They fill *always* and *forever* even as they find a home in your soul.

Prayer

Holy Blessed Trinity, offering me the graces of infinity, thank You.
Jesus, I trust in You.

June 5
A DECISION-MAKING CHECKLIST

Before each important action, I will stop to consider for
a moment what relationship it has to eternal life and
what may be the main reason for my undertaking it: is
it for the glory of God, or for the good of my own soul,
or for the good of the souls of others? (*Diary*, 1549)

Reflection

Any instructor or coach trying to teach a skill will stress the fundamentals. This little thing, followed by this little thing, followed by this little thing. And then demand those actions be done over and over and over. In a sense, our saints are instructors and coaches in holiness. On St. Faustina's list of basics is asking: Is what I'm considering doing for the glory of God? For the good of my soul? For the good of others' souls? They're questions to be asked again and again and again.

Prayer

Thank You, Heavenly Father, for providing such top-notch teachers and coaches to help me get my soul in shape.

Jesus, I trust in You.

June 6

BREAKFAST OF SAINTS

Every morning during meditation, I prepare myself for the whole day's struggle. Holy Communion assures me that I will win the victory; and so it is. I fear the day when I do not receive Holy Communion. This Bread of the Strong gives me all the strength I need to carry on my mission and the courage to do whatever the Lord asks of me. The courage and strength that are in me are not of me, but of Him who lives in me — it is the Eucharist. (*Diary*, 91)

Reflection

"The Bread of the Strong" isn't a common term for Holy Communion. It can put the Eucharist in a different light and, without being irreverent, has a bit of a ring to it like "Holy Communion, Breakfast of Saints." What better way to "prepare yourself for the whole day's struggle"?

Prayer

Thank You, Dear Lord, that on days I can't get to Mass and Communion You give me the opportunity to make a "Spiritual Communion." I want to do that more often. I want to start my day with You.

Jesus, I trust in You.

June 7
THE INSTRUMENTS OF JESUS

In order to purify a soul, Jesus uses whatever instruments
He likes. My soul underwent a complete abandonment
on the part of creatures; often my best intentions were
misinterpreted by the sisters, a type of suffering which is most
painful; but God allows it, and we must accept it because
in this way we become more like Jesus. (*Diary*, 38)

Reflection

As a carpenter, Jesus knew which tools to use on which woods. As
the Creator of your soul, He knows which "instruments" to use on
yours.

Prayer

Purify my soul, Dear Lord, by any means You see fit.
Jesus, I trust in You.

June 8

KEEPING IT SIMPLE

Patience, prayer and silence — these are what
give strength to the soul. (*Diary*, 944)

Reflection

Like any good teacher, St. Faustina knows sometimes it's best to
keep it simple. Let the students catch their breath and focus on
some basics. Although, perhaps with a class her third instruction
would come first: "Quiet down!" Then patiently, she and her class
would move on to prayer.

Prayer

Help me be more patient, Dear Lord. Help me be more prayerful.
Help me "to quiet down."

Jesus, I trust in You.

June 9

A NOT-SO-GREAT EXCUSE

> June 9, 1935. Pentecost. I understood that God demands
> a more perfect way of life of me. However, I kept using
> my incompetence as an excuse. (*Diary*, 435)

Reflection

No one could argue that the pre-Pentecost apostles were competent. Frightened and unsure, absolutely. Competent, not at that point. But then.... You know what happened. It astounded others in Jerusalem at the time, and it astounded the Twelve, too. What happened? They accepted the Holy Spirit and all He gave them despite their lack of competence, and confidence. With Him, they could do God's will. With Him, we can, too.

Prayer

Spirit of Pentecost, fill me with Your gifts, fruits, and graces ... despite my incompetence.

Jesus, I trust in You.

June 10
A NUN CALLED "DUMP"

My heart is always open to the sufferings of others; and I will not close my heart to the sufferings of others, even though because of this I have been scornfully nicknamed "dump"; that is, [because] everyone dumps his pain into my heart. [To this] I answered that everyone has a place in my heart and I, in return, have a place in the Heart of Jesus. (*Diary*, 871)

Reflection

Some of the little peeks St. Faustina gives of life in a convent are surprising. Her compassion for others led to her being "scornfully nicknamed 'dump.'" Wow! She figured it was worth it. A place in her heart for everyone; a place in the Sacred Heart for her. A wise lady.

Prayer

Dear Lord, help me earn the reputation of someone who is kind and caring to all. Not for my own glory, but for Yours.

Jesus, I trust in You.

June 11

WHY DOES GOD ALLOW ...?

In prayer I always find light and strength of spirit although there are moments so trying and hurtful, that it is sometimes difficult to imagine that these things can happen in a convent. Strangely, God sometimes allows them, but always in order to manifest or develop virtue in a soul. That is the reason for trials. (*Diary*, 166)

Reflection

It *is* strange that God allows some things to happen. Even steeped in belief, we just don't get it. Yes, those events may help us increase in virtue and knowledge, but the lessons are just so *hard*. Truly, His ways are not our ways, and learning to accept and follow His ways can be an uphill, twisting, rocky path.

Prayer

Heavenly Father, help me find light and strength of spirit during trying and hurtful times.

Jesus, I trust in You.

June 12

"PRAYER PALS"

Today Sister Jolanta asked me to make an agreement with her: she will pray for me, and I am to pray for the girls in her class in Vilnius. As for me, I always pray for our work, but I have resolved to pray for the class in Vilnius for two months, and Sister Jolanta will say three Hail Marys ... every day for the intention that I might profit from God's grace. Our friendship has deepened. (*Diary*, 1171)

Reflection

Those of us a certain age remember penpals. A friend made and kept by exchanging letters, often with someone on the other side of the country or the world. In today's quote, Sister Jolanta asks to be Sister Faustina's "prayer pal." What a profound idea. What's stopping us from asking the same of someone in our life?

Prayer

Dear Lord, please let me know if there's someone You want me to be "prayer pals" with.

Jesus, I trust in You.

June 13

"FOR MY FRIENDS ARE YOUR FRIENDS"

... God loves in a special way those whom we love. (*Diary*, 1438)

Reflection

An ancient fraternal order song (and now a children's ditty) sums up what St. Faustina writes: "The more we get together ... the happier we'll be. For my friends are your friends, and your friends are my friends. ..." It's such a human thing for God to do. Or such a godly thing for us to do. We have as special place in our heart, in our relationships, with those our Lord loves. And the ones we love deeply, the ones we pray for often, are loved by God in a particular way because of us. What a happy thought. What an amazing truth.

Prayer

Today, Dear Lord, I pray for N. and N. and N. and ... You know who they are. *Our* friends.

Jesus, I trust in You.

June 14

IN DRY TIMES

One hour spent at the foot of the altar in the greatest
dryness of spirit is dearer to me than a hundred
years of worldly pleasures. (*Diary*, 254)

Reflection

Today St. Faustina is telling us about her relationship with God.
She knows about, and has experienced, times of "dryness of spirit."
But even then her faith continued to assure her of the presence of
God on the altar—in the tabernacle—when any feelings on that
presence were absent.

Prayer

Deepen my faith and give me perseverance, Lord, when my prayer
life is dry. Help me remember and know You love me always.

Jesus, I trust in You.

June 15

A KEY TO THE KINGDOM

The moment I knelt down to cross out my own will, as the Lord had bid me to do, I heard this voice in my soul: **From today on, do not fear God's judgment, for you will not be judged.** (*Diary*, 374)

Reflection

Jesus handed St. Peter the keys of the Kingdom but He gives each of us one key *to* the Kingdom. It's this: The closer we get to doing God's will for us on earth, the closer we get to bypassing a stop in purgatory.

Prayer

Your will, Dear Heavenly Father. Your will.

Jesus, I trust in You.

June 16

HOLINESS AND THE RICHTER SCALE

> When my soul is in anguish, I think only in this way: Jesus is good and full of mercy, and even if the ground were to give way under my feet, I would not cease to trust in Him. (*Diary*, 1192)

Reflection

Those who live in earthquake-prone areas are no strangers to the Richter scale, a way of determining the magnitude of the event. Had St. Faustina heard of it? Possibly. The scale was first published in 1935 and St. Faustina died in 1938. We do know Poland had, and has, earthquakes. And we do know that, at times in our lives, it can feel as if the ground gave way under our feet. Not literally, but with a variety of life's personal disasters. Her advice? Don't "cease to trust in Him."

Prayer

Dear Lord, sometimes for so many, many reasons I'm afraid for myself and for others. Financial, medical, familial, spiritual … there are all kinds of "earthquakes." Divine Mercy, gentle Jesus, hold my hand.

Jesus, I trust in You.

June 17

A HEART LIKE HIS

Jesus, make my heart like unto Yours, or rather transform it into Your own Heart that I may sense the needs of other hearts, especially those who are sad and suffering. May the rays of mercy rest in my heart. (*Diary*, 514)

Reflection

St. Faustina shows the depth of her love for Jesus when she asks Him to make her heart more like — or even into — His to better "sense the needs of other hearts, especially those who are sad and suffering." Being more sympathetic — or harder still, being more empathetic — can take a toll. Yes, doing that includes praying for others but, closer to home, it can also mean *doing* something *for* others, including "just" listening.

Prayer

Dear Jesus, transform *my* heart into Your own heart. Let rays of mercy rest there, ready to serve those who are sad and suffering.

Jesus, I trust in You.

June 18

THE FIRE OF LOVE

Today is the Feast of the Most Sacred Heart of Jesus. During Holy Mass, I was given the knowledge of the Heart of Jesus and of the nature of the fire of love with which He burns for us and of how He is an Ocean of Mercy. (*Diary*, 1142)

Reflection

Once again St. Faustina uses striking images as she tries to tell us what she knows and believes. The love of Christ for her is a fire, and at the same time, His mercy is an ocean. That's true for us, too. The same Christ, the same love, the same mercy. That's how He loves you. That's the endless amount of mercy He has for you.

Prayer

(From the Litany of the Sacred Heart)
Heart of Jesus, burning furnace of charity, have mercy on us. *Heart of Jesus*, abode of justice and love, have mercy on us. *Heart of Jesus*, full of goodness and love, have mercy on us. *Heart of Jesus*, abyss of all virtues, have mercy on us. *Heart of Jesus*, most worthy of all praise, have mercy on us. *Heart of Jesus*, King and center of all hearts, have mercy on us.

Jesus, I trust in You.

June 19

IN THE FINAL STRIFE

> O Mary, my sweet Mother,
> To You I turn over my soul, my body and my poor heart.
> Be the guardian of my life,
> Especially at the hour of death in the final fight. (*Diary*, 161)

Reflection

Imagine what a difference it will make if, at the hour of our death, at the moment of our "final strife," our Blessed Mother is with us. If your Blessed Mother is with you.

Prayer

Today, Dear Mary, please be with all those who are dying. And please be near their loved ones. Immaculate Heart of Mary, keep us in your care!

Jesus, I trust in You.

June 20

WHEN THE HONEYMOON IS OVER

Pure love is capable of great deeds, and it is not broken by difficulty or adversity. As it remains strong in the midst of great difficulties, so too it perseveres in the toilsome and drab life of each day. It knows that only one thing is needed to please God: to do even the smallest things out of great love—love, and always love. (*Diary*, 140)

Reflection

St. Faustina probably didn't know what she was describing is that period in a marriage when "the honeymoon is over." It always comes and, as she writes, love can overcome it. Any close relationship has times of difficulty and adversity. It, too, has to persevere "in the toilsome and drab life of each day." Human love may not conquer all but it conquers a lot. And, another topic, how to please God? What we need is to love.

Prayer

Dear Lord, help me worry less and love more.

Jesus, I trust in You.

June 21

CONFESSION: DON'T LEAVE EARTH WITHOUT IT

At that moment, a ray of light illumined my soul, and I saw the whole abyss of my misery. In that same moment I nestled close to the Most Sacred Heart of Jesus with so much trust that even if I had the sins of all the damned weighing on my conscience, I would not have doubted God's mercy but, with a heart crushed to dust, I would have thrown myself into the abyss of Your mercy. I believe, O Jesus, that you would not reject me, but would absolve me through the hand of Your representative. (*Diary*, 1318)

Reflection

Today's quote is a strong endorsement for the sacrament of confession. Even if the sins "of all the damned" weighed on St. Faustina's conscience, she had no doubt" Divine Mercy would forgive it all "through the hand of Your representative." At a parish near you.

Prayer

Thank You for the sacrament of confession, Lord. Help me take better advantage of what You so generously offer me. Time and time again.

Jesus, I trust in You.

June 22

ZIP THE LIPS, OPEN THE EARS

The mercy of God, hidden in the Blessed Sacrament, the voice of the Lord who speaks to us from the throne of mercy: **Come to Me, all of you.** (*Diary*, 1485)

Reflection

We have to talk a *lot* less and listen a *lot* more to hear Our Lord speaking to us as He calls, "Come to Me." And we have to spend time with the Eucharistic Lord just as St. Faustina did. Now, we probably can't match the number of hours she did that but, yes, we can increase the time that we kneel before, and sit with, Jesus hidden in the Blessed Sacrament. Even if it's just for a few minutes. Or only for a moment or two.

Prayer

The Body of Christ. Amen. I believe, Lord, I believe.

Jesus, I trust in You.

June 23
INFLATED WITH PRIDE

How can one be pleasing to God when one is inflated with pride and self-love under the pretense of striving for God's glory, while in fact one is seeking one's own glory? (*Diary*, 1139)

Reflection

Better to be like St. John the Baptist: "He must increase, but I must decrease" (Jn 3:30).

Prayer

All praise, all honor, all glory to You, Dear Lord. Today, and always. Jesus, I trust in You.

June 24

LESS ME, MORE YOU

I have come to know that, in order for God to act in a soul, it must give up acting on its own; otherwise, God will not carry out His will in it. (*Diary*, 1790)

Reflection

St. Faustina is saying what St. John the Baptist said so long ago: "He must increase, but I must decrease" (Jn 3:30). A basic truth simply stated. The challenge of a lifetime. A challenge for each of us today.

Prayer

Holy Spirit, I want to become better at "less me, more You." Fill me with Your gifts to help me do that.

Jesus, I trust in You.

June 25

DIVINE HIDE-AND-GO-SEEK

My heart is drawn there where my God is hidden,
Where He dwells with us day and night,
Clothed in the White Host;
He governs the whole world, He communes
with souls. (*Diary*, 1591)

Reflection

God can be so easy to see, through the eyes of faith. And so hard to find, through the eyes of pride. So silent, unless we pause to listen. So absent, unless we choose to move closer, to be closer, to Him. Christ the King is "clothed in the White Host." The Prince of Peace offers us the opportunity to serve Him in "the least among us" (see Mt 25:31–46). What a difference receiving Communion more reverently, of being more generous to those in need, would have in our vision. In our finding our "hidden" God.

Prayer

Lord, help me see better today. You in the Blessed Sacrament. You in others in need. You … who are with me "day and night." With me always.

Jesus, I trust in You.

June 26

ONE SMALL SPARK

I desire, O my Jesus, to suffer and burn with the flame of Your love in all the circumstances of my life. I am Yours, completely Yours, and I wish to disappear in You, O Jesus, I wish to be lost in Your divine beauty. You pursue me with Your love, O Lord; You penetrate my soul like a ray of the sun and change its darkness into Your light. I feel very vividly that I am living in You as one small spark swallowed up by the incomprehensible fire with which You burn, O inconceivable Trinity! (*Diary*, 507)

Reflection

Jesus, I know You're calling me to be the light set on a lampstand to give light to the whole house. To my family, to my friends, to all those with whom I come into contact today. With Your help, in Your name, I want to do that.

Prayer

Divine Light, be with me — one small spark — today.

Jesus, I trust in You.

June 27

ST. FAUSTINA AND ST. PAUL

My Jesus, I understand well that my perfection consists not in the fact that You command me to carry out these great works of Yours—Oh no!—the soul's greatness does not consist in this, but in great love for You. O Jesus, in the depths of my soul I understand that the greatest achievements cannot compare with one act of pure love for You. (*Diary*, 984)

Reflection

In today's quote, in her prayer to Jesus, St. Faustina is saying what St. Paul said. "If I speak in the tongues of men and of angels, but have not love, I am a noisy gong or a clanging cymbal. And if I have prophetic powers, and understand all mysteries and all knowledge, and if I have all faith, so as to remove mountains, but have not love, I am nothing. If I give away all I have, and if I deliver my body to be burned, but have not love, I gain nothing" (1 Cor 13:1–3). The lesson from both? We will be judged on how we loved.

Prayer

Help me love You, and others, more, Dear Lord. Help me live that love daily.

Jesus, I trust in You.

June 28

A LITTLE LISTENING

Oh, if souls would only be willing to listen, at least a little,
to the voice of conscience and the voice—that is, the
inspirations—of the Holy Spirit! I say "at least a little," because
once we open ourselves to the influence of the Holy Spirit,
He himself will fulfill what is lacking in us. (*Diary*, 359)

Reflection

It's frustrating when we offer the answer but nobody pays attention
to what we're saying. St. Faustina sounds like that in today's quote.
If folks would just listen—even a little bit!—to what the Holy
Spirit is telling them then.... They, we, would find what is "lacking
in us."

Prayer

Let's spend a little quiet time together right now, Holy Spirit.
Jesus, I trust in You.

June 29

COMPLETELY LOVES YOU

Today, I saw the Sacred Heart of Jesus in the sky, in the midst of a great brilliance. The rays were issuing from the Wound [in His side] and spreading out over the entire world. (*Diary*, 1796)

Reflection

It was the angels that told the shepherds what had happened in that stable, about the Savior. It was the star that led the Magi to the Infant Jesus, the King. It was the Sacred Heart of Jesus that drove home the point for St. Faustina that through His wounds He touches the entire world. Savior, King, Sacred Heart. True God and true man. Came for all. Came for you. Died for all. Died for you. Completely loves all. Completely loves you. How can realizing that change my life ... today?

Prayer

Lord, by Your life, death, and resurrection, you have set me free. I want to use that freedom wisely ... for You.

Jesus, I trust in You.

June 30

THANK YOU, LORD

Thank You, O Lord, for creating me,
For calling me into being from nothingness,
For imprinting Your divinity on my soul,
The work of sheer merciful love. (*Diary*, 1286)

Reflection

Sometimes the best way to thank God is to treat His sons and daughters better.

Prayer

You created me from nothingness and made me Your beloved child. You placed Your very presence within my soul. Oh, thank You, my Dear, Sweet, Heavenly Father.

Jesus, I trust in You.

CHAPTER SEVEN

Reflections

FOR

July

July 1
WITH HIM

With Him I go to work, with Him I go for recreation, with Him I suffer, with Him I rejoice; I live in Him and He in me. I am never alone, because He is my constant companion. He is present to me at every moment. Our intimacy is very close, through a union of blood and of life. (*Diary*, 318)

Reflection

St. Faustina offers such a wonderful, and comforting, image of how we can view our day. Through this, that, and the other, we're never alone. Through every moment, we are "with Him." All day and all night long, He is with us.

Prayer

Today, Dear Lord, and tonight, let those who feel lonely or abandoned know that You're with them. Help them feel Your peace and Your presence "at every moment."

Jesus, I trust in You.

July 2
WITH HOOK AND THREAD

This morning after completing my spiritual exercises, I began at once to crochet. I sensed a stillness in my heart; I sensed that Jesus was resting in it. That deep and sweet consciousness of God's presence prompted me to say to the Lord, "O Most Holy Trinity dwelling in my heart, I beg You: grant the grace of conversion to as many souls as the [number of] stitches that I will make today with this crochet hook." (*Diary*, 961)

Reflection

It seems safe to speculate St. Faustina wasn't crocheting something for herself but for the community or others. Even so, there's a sense of leisure-time activity. Of a body resting, of a mind gently wandering, and of a soul praying. We need that, too. That slowing down, that soothing activity, that stillness in our heart. It's a time, a place, and a way God can speak to *us*.

Prayer

Thank You for hobbies, Jesus. Thank You for leisure-time activities. Thank You for "resting" in my heart.

Jesus, I trust in You.

July 3

A PRAYER OF HEALING

When I received Holy Communion, I don't know why, but it was as if something were urging me to this prayer, and I began to pray in this manner: "Jesus, may Your pure and healthy blood circulate in my ailing organism, and may Your pure and healthy body transform my weak body, and may a healthy and vigorous life throb within me, if it is truly Your holy will that I should set about the work in question; and this will be a clear sign of Your holy will for me." (*Diary*, 1089)

Reflection

In today's quote it seems that St. Faustina is asking for a "Jesus transfusion" for better physical health. Not for the sake of health itself but so she'll know if she's to do what she thinks Our Lord may be asking her to do. Something that's beyond her physical abilities right now. It's a faith-filled and deeply spiritual way to better discern what God's will is. It's a method, a prayer, we can use ourselves.

Prayer

Heavenly Father, if You're asking me to do something, please let me know it and give me the strength to do it. If You're not asking that, help me humbly accept my limitations.

Jesus, I trust in You.

July 4
THROUGH THE WOUNDS OF JESUS

On one occasion I heard these words in my soul. **Make a novena for your country. This novena will consist of the recitation of the Litany of the Saints....** Towards the end of the litany I saw a great radiance and, in the midst of it, God the Father. Between this radiance and the earth I saw Jesus, nailed to the Cross in such a way that when God wanted to look at the earth, He had to look through the wounds of Jesus. And I understood that it was for the sake of Jesus that God blesses the earth. (*Diary*, 59–60)

Reflection

What a powerful image. God sees the world, God sees you, "through the wounds of Jesus." He sees you through Christ's sacrifice and love. He sees you through Divine Mercy.

Prayer

Oh, Dear Heavenly Father, I want to get better at seeing others as You see me.

Jesus, I trust in You.

July 5
KNOWING MYSELF

Jesus, Supreme Light, grant me the grace of knowing myself, and pierce my dark soul with Your light, and fill the abyss of my soul with Your own self ... (*Diary*, 297)

Reflection

What a wonderful thing to get to know ourselves better, and so better see how our Creator is always with us. Ready to fill our hearts, our minds, and our souls.

Prayer

Light of the World, fill me with the light of life.

Jesus, I trust in You.

July 6

ALL WHO DIE TODAY

Jesus, I beg You, by the inconceivable power of Your mercy,
that all the souls who will die today escape the fire of hell,
even if they have been the greatest sinners. (*Diary*, 873)

Reflection

By our prayers and sacrifices, we—on this day and every
day—have the power, the gift from God, to play a role in influenc-
ing the eternity of others.

Prayer

I pray, Divine Mercy, for all who will die today. May all those souls,
each Your child, be given the grace to live with You forever.

Jesus, I trust in You.

July 7
JUST A "PINCH" OF SIN

In the meditation on sin, the Lord gave me to know all the malice of sin and the ingratitude that is contained in it. I feel within my soul a great aversion for even the smallest sin. (*Diary*, 1334)

Reflection

Today St. Faustina is saying a sin is a sin is a sin. From the biggest to the smallest they contain — what we might call — "the same DNA." Yes, different seriousness, effects, and consequences, but in each the same grains of "ingratitude." The same "Forget it, God. I'm doing what *I* want to do." The same turning from Love Itself.

Prayer

I want to choose love, Lord. I want to choose You. Always.
   Jesus, I trust in You.

July 8
KNOW MORE, KNOW LESS

Oh, if I could only cut my heart into tiny pieces and in this way offer to You, O Jesus, each piece as a heart whole and entire, to make up in part for the hearts that do not love You! I love You, Jesus, with every drop of my blood, and I would gladly shed my blood for You to give You a proof of the sincerity of my love. O God, the more I know You the less I can comprehend You, but this "non-comprehension" lets me realize how great You are! (*Diary*, 57)

Reflection

In the first part of today's quote St. Faustina is pouring out her love for her Groom. (It sounds very much like a young woman pouring her heart out on paper to a young gentleman.) But the second part of today's quote is a little more feet-planted-on-the-ground: the more I know You the more I realize I can never fully understand You. It's what happens when we bump up against, or fall deeply in love with, the Infinite.

Prayer

I'd like to get to know You a little better, Lord. A lot better really but — I suspect — that happens a little bit at a time.

Jesus, I trust in You.

July 9
NOISY EMOTIONS

It is no easy thing to bear sufferings joyfully, especially those which are unmerited. Fallen nature rebels, and although the intellect and will are above suffering, because they are able to do good to those who inflict suffering on them, nevertheless the emotions raise a lot of noise and, like restless spirits, attack the intellect and will. But when they see they cannot do anything by themselves, they quiet down and submit to the intellect and will. Like some kind of hideousness, they rush in and stir up a row, bent on making one obey them alone so long as they are not curbed by the intellect and will. (*Diary*, 1152)

Reflection

"Emotions raise a lot of noise." They "attack the intellect and will." We *know* better. We want to *do* better but.... We can take heart in the fact that those negative emotions don't last, that they have no staying power, unless we give it to them. Unless we fall into the habit of letting them rule who we are.

Prayer

Our Lady, Queen of Peace, help me stay calm when my emotions urge me to charge forward in anger. Be with me then, Dear Mother. Be with me. Help me be your child of peace.

Jesus, I trust in You.

July 10

IN SUCH A STATE

There are times in life when a soul is in such a state that it does not seem to understand human speech. Everything tires it, and nothing but ardent prayer will put it at ease. In fervent prayer the soul finds relief and, even if it wanted explanation from creatures, these would only make it more restless. (*Diary*, 1387)

Reflection

Our mind can be in a frenzy, our heart can race, our very soul can be "in such a state" when life's challenges—and fears—overwhelm us. Small wonder we're exhausted. That's a time for prayer, St. Faustina says. For "ardent prayer." That doesn't necessarily mean long prayers. Or prayer before the Blessed Sacrament. It can be as simple, as powerful, and as comforting as: "Jesus, I trust in You."

Prayer

Right now, Dear Lord, bring comfort to those who are "in such a state." Ease their minds, quiet their hearts, and help them know You are with them. Always.

Jesus, I trust in You.

July 11

THROUGH SUFFERING

Today the Lord Jesus is giving me an awareness of Himself and of His most tender love and care for me. He is bringing me to understand deeply how everything depends on His will, and how He allows certain difficulties precisely for our merit, so that our fidelity might be clearly manifest. And through this, I have been given strength for suffering and self-denial. (*Diary*, 1409)

Reflection

No, Jesus isn't giving us some kind of test. He's offering us a way to grow stronger in our love and faith. To be better able to offer deeper sympathy, and sometimes even empathy, to those who suffer.

Prayer

Dear Lord, I know that everything You give me is good. But, sometimes, it's so hard.

Jesus, I trust in You.

July 12
THE CHAPLET FOR RAIN

The heat is so intense today that it is difficult to bear. We are all thirsting for rain, and still it does not come. For several days the sky has been overcast, but there is no rain. When I looked at the plants, thirsting for the rain I was moved with pity, and I decided to say the chaplet until the Lord would send us rain. Before supper, the sky covered over with clouds, and a heavy rain fell on the earth. I had been saying this prayer without interruption for three hours. And the Lord let me know that everything can be obtained by means of this prayer. (*Diary*, 1128)

Reflection

It's easy to imagine Jesus was greatly pleased with St. Faustina for so diligently—religiously!—using the chaplet He had given her. Yes, prayers for the wilting plants, but more so for community members and others who found the intense heat so difficult to bear. Like the woman in The Parable of the Widow and the Unjust Judge (see Lk 18:1–8), the young nun *just did not let up*. No doubt her prayers of thanksgiving began with the first small raindrops.

Prayer

Heavenly Father, help me ask, and ask, and ask for good things for others and myself. For things that are a part of Your will for us.

Jesus, I trust in You.

July 13
PROTECTING CHILDREN

On one occasion, [in a vision] I saw ... a crowd of children who seemed to be no older than five to eleven years of age. When they saw me they surrounded me and began to cry out, "Defend us from evil," and they led me into the chapel which was in this convent. When I entered the chapel, I saw the distressful Lord Jesus. Jesus looked at me graciously and said ... **You are to defend them from evil. From that moment, I have been praying for children, but I feel that prayer alone is not enough.** (*Diary*, 765)

Reflection

St. Faustina makes an important point when it comes to protecting children, a topic that dominates the news in our own time. Yes, we need to keep them in our prayers, but "that alone is not enough." We're also called to take action to keep them safe from those who would harm them.

Prayer

Dear Lord Jesus, bless the children. Help all of us protect them with our prayers and our actions.

Jesus, I trust in You.

July 14

WITH HANDS FULL

Help me, O Lord, that my hands may be merciful and filled with good deeds, so that I may do only good to my neighbors and take upon myself the more difficult and toilsome tasks. (*Diary*, 163)

Reflection

What's to be the "work of [my] human hands," to adapt a phrase from the Offertory of the Mass? What acts of mercy and good deeds remain undone, waiting for me to do them? For me in particular, for me alone, with the One who has given me these hands.

Prayer

Heavenly Father, into Your hands I commend my hands. I am Yours.

Jesus, I trust in You.

July 15

IN A FLOWER BLOSSOM

I want to hide myself in Your Most Merciful Heart as a dewdrop does in a flower blossom. Enclose me in this blossom against the frost of the world. No one can conceive the happiness which my heart enjoys in its solitude, alone with God. (*Diary*, 1395)

Reflection

St. Faustina — at times the community's gardener — uses images with which she's familiar. She wants to be like a dewdrop in a flower blossom. A child of God tucked away in His Most Merciful Heart. So content, so safe, so loved and in love. Today, and always, *you* are that dewdrop. *You* can experience spending time alone with your God.

Prayer

Thank You, Dear Lord, for spending time with me, and for letting me spend time with You.

Jesus, I trust in You.

July 16

"FAIR-HEALTH" FRIENDS

It often happens when one is ill, as in the case of Job in the Old Testament, that as long as one can move about and work, everything is fine and dandy; but when God sends illness, somehow or other, there are fewer friends about. But yet, there are some. They still take interest in our suffering and all that, but if God sends a longer illness, even those faithful friends slowly begin to desert us. They visit us less frequently, and often their visits cause suffering. Instead of comforting us, they reproach us about certain things, which is an occasion of a good deal of suffering. And so the soul, like Job, is alone; but fortunately, it is not alone, because Jesus-Host is with it. (*Diary*, 1509)

Reflection

We're familiar with the term "fair-weather friends" but St. Faustina is talking about fair-health friends. Happy to help ... for a time ... when we have health troubles. But then they wonder, aren't we better yet? Two points to consider. One, Jesus is an always-friend. And, two, how do we treat those around us who have chronic conditions, or conditions that are difficult to diagnose?

Prayer

Help me be patient with a friend who's sick, Dear Lord. And help me be patient with my friends when I'm sick.

Jesus, I trust in You.

July 17
THANKS, BUT ...

My Jesus, how good and patient You are! You often look upon us as little children. We often beg You, but we don't know what for, because towards the end of the prayer, when You give us what we have asked for, we do not want to accept it. (*Diary*, 1524)

Reflection

Aren't we fickle children of God? Asking, and finally getting; and then saying, "No, thanks." Perhaps (our patient) God is hoping we'll learn to ask for what's best for us. Ask for what He wants us to have, what He's always wanted for us.

Prayer

What do I want today, Dear Lord? Surprise me. You know best.
Jesus, I trust in You.

July 18

REVIEWING A BASIC

The essence of the virtues is the will of God. He who does the will of God faithfully, practices all the virtues. (*Diary*, 678)

Reflection

One of St. Faustina's major themes is doing God's will. She comes at it from a lot of different angles but her point is always the same. Do it! How, for example? Practice "all the virtues." (And, of course, obey the Ten Commandments.)

Prayer

Help me be your good student, Dear St. Faustina, and learn this lesson. And learn to live this lesson.

Jesus, I trust in You.

July 19

SURROUNDED BY "ANGELS"

Oh, how sweet it is to live in a convent among sisters, but I must not forget that these angels are in human bodies. (*Diary*, 1126)

Reflection

In today's quote St. Faustina has high praise for her fellow sisters and is so pleased to be a member of the congregation. But ... she doesn't lose sight of the fact these "angels" are human and there's always bound to be some friction.

Prayer

Thank You, Dear Lord, for the wonderful friends and family members You've put in my life. Forgive us for the times we ... clash.

Jesus, I trust in You.

July 20
PAST, PRESENT, AND FUTURE

When I look into the future, I am frightened,
But why plunge into the future?
Only the present moment is precious to me,
As the future may never enter my soul at all.

It is no longer in my power,
To change, correct or add to the past;
For neither sages nor prophets could do that.
And so, what the past has embraced I
must entrust to God. (*Diary*, 2)

Reflection

We tend to be time travelers when it comes to worries and regrets.
That's so even though the One who created time tells us to focus on
here and now. To "let the day's own trouble be sufficient for the day"
(Mt 6:34). That takes prayer ... and practice.

Prayer

Oh, Dear Lord, don't let me get mired in the past or caught up in
the future. Help me remember *this* is the day You made, a time to
rejoice and be glad.

Jesus, I trust in You.

July 21

DEEP PEACE

My soul was filled with a peace much deeper than anything I had experienced before, a divine reassurance which nothing can efface, a deep peace which nothing can disturb, even though I were to go through the severest of ordeals. I am at peace; God Himself governs all things. (*Diary*, 1660)

Reflection

"Rejoice in the Lord always; again I will say, Rejoice. Let all men know your forbearance. The Lord is at hand. Have no anxiety about anything, but in everything by prayer and supplication with thanksgiving let your requests be made known to God. And the peace of God, which passes all understanding, will keep your hearts and your minds in Christ Jesus" (Phil 4:4–7).

Prayer

Thank You, Lord, that I don't have to understand Your peace in order to receive it.

Jesus, I trust in You.

July 22

A NIAGARA FALLS OF MERCY

O Blood and Water, which gushed forth from the Heart of Jesus as a fount of mercy for us, I trust in You! (*Diary*, 84)

Reflection

We tend to think of a "fount" as a quiet spring or delicate water fountain. But St. Faustina said Christ's blood and water "gushed" from the His heart. In that sense, it's a Niagara Falls of love, a flooded river of grace, a tsunami of forgiveness. It can knock us over, sweep us away, and lift us higher and higher … and closer and closer to Him.

Prayer

Dear Jesus, I am at Your mercy. Thank God.

Jesus, I trust in You.

July 23

> Spiritual Counsel Given to Me by Father Andrasz, S.J.: "Act in such a way that all those who come in contact with you will go away joyful. Sow happiness about you because you have received much from God; give, then, generously to others. They should take leave of you with their hearts filled with joy, even if they have no more than touched the hem of your garment." (*Diary*, 55)

Reflection

What if today those with whom we come into contact go away a little happier? Father Andrasz is saying it doesn't take much, just being a bit more generous and kind.

Prayer

Dear Lord, today I want to be a "sower of happiness."

Jesus, I trust in You.

July 24

If we live in this spirit of mercy, we ourselves
will obtain mercy. (*Diary*, 550)

Reflection

Here St. Faustina borrows a line from Jesus' Sermon on the Mount.
"Blessed are the merciful, for they shall obtain mercy" (Mt 5:7). It's
a truth that bears repeating. To ourselves. Often.

Prayer

Lord, have mercy on me for the times I've been unmerciful. Christ,
I want to live in "a spirit of mercy." Lord, I forgive those who have
shown little or no mercy to me.

Jesus, I trust in You.

July 25
WITH THE BEST OF INTENTIONS

> If one does not know what is better, one must reflect, consider and seek advice, because one must not act with an uncertain conscience. When uncertain, say to yourself: "Whatever I do will be good. I have the intention of doing good." The Lord God accepts what we consider good, and the Lord God also accepts and considers it as good. One should not worry if, after some time, one sees that these things are not good. God looks at the intention with which we begin, and will reward us accordingly. This is a principle which we ought to follow. (*Diary*, 800)

Reflection

Again, St. Faustina is very specific in what's she recommending to herself and for herself. To us and for us. Here, it's comforting to know that if we make a poor decision based on a good intention, that's all right with God. What's a "good intention"? Most simply put, it's the desire to do good.

Prayer

Thanks, Dear Lord, for caring about *why* I do something, especially when the results are … not so good.

Jesus, I trust in You.

July 26
MULTIPLE DEFINITIONS

> Jesus gave me to know the depth of His meekness
> and humility and to understand that He clearly
> demanded the same of me. (*Diary*, 758)

Reflection

Maybe we bristle a bit at "meekness" and "humility" because we equate them with being a doormat: anyone can walk all over us. But, certainly, that's not what Jesus demands because it's not why God created us. "Meek" can mean no spirit or courage. But it can mean enduring injury with patience and without resentment. "Humble" can mean insignificant. But it can mean not being proud, haughty, or arrogant. We know how Jesus was meek and humble. And so we know how He wants us to be this way, too.

Prayer

Thank You, Dear Jesus, for showing us what You were teaching us by living those lessons.

Jesus, I trust in You.

July 27
A PLACE PERMEATED WITH GOD

When I was attending Mass in a certain church with another sister, I felt the greatness and majesty of God; I felt the church was permeated by God. His majesty enveloped me and, though it terrified me, it filled me with peace and joy. I knew that nothing could oppose His will. Oh, if only all souls knew who is living in our churches, there would not be so many outrages and so much disrespect in these holy places! (*Diary*, 409)

Reflection

In a land and at a time without the royalty that was once at the center of past ages, it can be harder to imagine the majesty afforded those leaders. The wealth, the power, the influence. In today's quote St. Faustina writes of being overwhelmed by God's majesty. How often do we consider that? How often do we speak to Him and thank Him as the King of kings and Lord of lords?

Prayer

Dear God of greatness and majesty, fill me—Your servant—with Your love. Fill me—Your child—with Your peace and joy.

Jesus, I trust in You.

July 28

IN STORMS, SUFFERINGS, AND TRIALS

O my Lord, inflame my heart with love for You, that
my spirit may not grow weary amidst the storms,
the sufferings and the trials. (*Diary*, 94)

Reflection

"Weary" is tired weighed down with exhaustion. It can last day after
day and through sleepless night after sleepless night. Life's storms,
sufferings, and trials can wear us down to the point that we ask,
"Where are You, Lord?" But like the Israelites in the desert being
led by a pillar of fire during the night, like the Magi following a star
to find the Christ Child, Jesus can "inflame" our heart with a love
for Him. And that makes all the difference in the world.

Prayer

Rest with me, Lord, when I'm so very tired. Then take me by the
hand and help me rise.

Jesus, I trust in You.

July 29

IN YOUR DEPTHS

O Wound of Mercy, Heart of Jesus, hide me in Your depths
as a drop of Your own blood, and do not let me out forever!
Lock me in Your depths, and do You Yourself teach me to
love You! Eternal Love, do You Yourself form my soul that
it be made capable of returning Your love. (*Diary*, 1631)

Reflection

We know that blood transfusions save lives. What St. Faustina is
saying is that it can save souls, too. If our blood — our being — becomes so deeply mingled with Christ's we become "capable of
returning His love." We become better able to love all, just as He
does.

Prayer

Sacred Heart of Jesus, Most Precious Blood, thank You for coming
to me in the Holy Eucharist.

Jesus, I trust in You.

July 30

CRAZY IN LOVE

O Jesus, eternal God, thank You for Your countless graces and blessings. Let every beat of my heart be a new hymn of thanksgiving to You, O God. Let every drop of my blood circulate for You, Lord. My soul is one hymn in adoration of Your mercy. I love You, God, for Yourself alone. (*Diary*, 1794)

Reflection

Today St. Faustina's words sound like a modern-day pop song. With every beat of her heart. With every drop of her blood. As a young woman flat-out crazy in love. Which she was. With Jesus. Why? Not because she had lost her mind, but because her soul had become "one hymn in adoration of Your mercy."

Prayer

Today, Dear Lord, I want to love You more, and with more fervor. Help my soul become a "hymn of adoration to You." Today, I join St. Faustina in thanking "You for Your countless graces and blessings."

Jesus, I trust in You.

July 31

SHARING YOUR FAITH

O God, how I desire that souls come to know You and to see that You have created them because of Your unfathomable love. O my Creator and Lord, I feel that I am going to remove the veil of heaven so that earth will not doubt Your goodness. (*Diary*, 483)

Reflection

How to help others come to know God? Let them "see" Him through your beliefs, your faith, lived daily. Let your actions speak your words.

Prayer

Divine Mercy, today I pray for those who can't see through the "veil of heaven." Please, let them see You, the Light of Life, shining through that veil, and in their lives.

Jesus, I trust in You.

CHAPTER EIGHT

Reflections

FOR

August

August 1
"JUST WHAT I AM"

> O my Jesus, You know that there are times when I have neither lofty thoughts nor a soaring spirit. I bear with myself patiently and admit that that is just what I am, because all that is beautiful is a grace from God. And so I humble myself profoundly and cry out for Your help; and the grace of visitation is not slow in coming to the humble heart. (*Diary*, 1734)

Reflection

Sometimes when we pray we're just ... sort of there. No "lofty thoughts" or "soaring spirit." Even then, and maybe especially then, God is ready to come to us, to enter our own "humble heart." To be with us, just as we are.

Prayer

Help me keep my heart humble, Dear Jesus, and fill it with Your love.

Jesus, I trust in You.

August 2

A TORN HEART

Today, I experienced a great suffering during the visit of our sisters. I learned of something that hurt me terribly, but I controlled myself so that the sisters didn't notice anything. For some time, the pain was tearing my heart apart, but all that is for the sake of poor sinners.... O Jesus, for poor sinners.... Jesus, my strength, stay close to me, help me ... (*Diary*, 875)

Reflection

Again, St. Faustina is reminding us that her life was like ours: not all sunshine and roses. Like her, sometimes we're deeply hurt by what others say. Yes, at times we're called to speak up, to call them on it, but at other times we can only accept the pain "tearing" our heart apart and offer it up for others.

Prayer

Dear Lord, God of Divine Mercy, forgive me for the times I've torn apart the hearts of others by what I said or did. If possible, help me go to them and offer my apologies.

Jesus, I trust in You.

August 3

NO SMALL POTATOES

… [I]n the wards' kitchen, I was very upset because I could not manage the pots [of potatoes], which were very large…. At noon, during the examination of conscience, I complained to God about my weakness. Then I heard the following words in my soul. **From today on you will do this easily; I shall strengthen you.** That evening, when the time came to drain off the water from the potatoes, I hurried to be the first to do it, trusting in the Lord's words. I took up the pot with ease and poured off the water perfectly. But when I took off the cover … I saw there in the pot, in the place of the potatoes, whole bunches of red roses, beautiful beyond description. I had never seen such roses before… I heard a voice within me saying, **I change such hard work of yours into bouquets of most beautiful flowers, and their perfume rises up to My throne.** (*Diary*, 65)

Reflection

Two points: First, notice that St. Faustina offered a "prayer of complaint." And second, God wants to help us in *everything*. Nothing we ask of Him is just "small potatoes."

Prayer

Thank You, Heavenly Father, that I can talk to You about everything. And that You listen.

Jesus, I trust in You.

August 4

GOD THE ADVISOR

When I hesitate on how to act in some situations. I always ask Love. It advises best. (*Diary*, 1354)

Reflection

When we're in need of wisdom and counsel, when we're unsure what to do, who better to turn to than the Holy Spirit? Who better than God, who *is* Love?

Prayer

Holy Spirit, please give me the wisdom to always choose what most pleases You.

Jesus, I trust in You.

August 5

APPARENT OBSTACLES

August 5, 1935. Then I saw the Blessed Virgin, unspeakably beautiful. She came down from the altar to my kneeler, held me close to herself and said to me, *I am Mother to you all, thanks to the unfathomable mercy of God. Most pleasing to Me is that soul which faithfully carries out the will of God. . . . Be courageous. Do not fear apparent obstacles, but fix your gaze upon the Passion of My Son, and in this way you will be victorious.* (Diary, 449)

Reflection

What a comforting message of advice and encouragement Mary shares with her beloved daughter, or son. Do the will of God. Be brave. Don't be afraid of bumps in the road . . . or mountains to climb. Remember Christ's Passion and you will *win!*

Prayer

Dear sweet, beautiful Mary, hold me close. Protect me with your motherly mantle.

Jesus, I trust in You.

August 6

IN THE PEWS

Jesus has made known to me that I should pray for the sisters who are making the retreat. During prayer, I learned of the struggle that some are undergoing, and I redoubled my prayers. (*Diary*, 1335)

Reflection

For St. Faustina it was her fellow sisters on a retreat. For us it can be fellow parishioners at Sunday Mass. How often do we pray for them … right then, right there? Most likely we know only a few details, but we can be sure of this: each is "undergoing struggles."

Prayer

Today, Dear Lord, I pray for all the members of my parish and, in a particular way, for the staff, deacon, and especially our pastor.

Jesus, I trust in You.

August 7

LIE DETECTOR TEST

There is a certain person ... who tests my patience. I must devote much time to her. When I talk with her, I feel that she is lying, and this, continually.... But I am inwardly convinced that there is no truth in what she says. When it occurred to me once that I might be mistaken and that she might be telling the truth, I asked the Lord Jesus to give me the following sign: if she is really lying, let her admit to me herself that she has lied about any one of the things concerning which I am inwardly convinced that she is lying. And if she is telling the truth, let the Lord Jesus take this conviction away from me. A little later, she came to me again and said, "Sister, I beg your forgiveness, but I have lied about such and such a thing," and I understood that the inner light concerning that person had not misled me. (*Diary*, 901)

Reflection

Liars (embellishers, prevaricators) can test our patience, too. We have a choice. Not over their actions, but ours. We can choose to be honest. Always. Including when we need to tell the truth ... gently.

Prayer

Thanks for always being honest with me, Lord. Even when I don't like hearing—or admitting—it.

Jesus, I trust in You.

August 8
A SPIRITUAL POWERHOUSE

In a suffering soul we should see Jesus Crucified, and not a loafer or burden on the community. A soul who suffers with submission to the will of God draws down more blessings on the whole convent than all the working sisters. Poor indeed is a convent where there are no sick sisters. God often grants many and great graces out of regard for the souls who are suffering, and He withholds many punishments solely because of the suffering souls. (*Diary*, 1268)

Reflection

Today St. Faustina has a message for you if you're sick, elderly, disabled, or frail: *you* are a spiritual powerhouse for others. Those who are healthy and strong rely on you far more than any of us can possibly know or imagine. Out of His regard for *you*, God often grants many and great graces to your family, friends, parish, and neighborhood. Your power and influence are worldwide, and like no other.

Prayer

Thank You, Lord, for those whose suffering is a prayer for others. Let them know this, and let it bring them comfort.

Jesus, I trust in You.

August 9
GOD WITHIN ME

When some suffering afflicts me, it no longer causes
me any bitterness, nor do great consolations carry me
away. I am filled with the peace and equanimity that
flow from the knowledge of the truth.

How can living surrounded by unfriendly hearts do me any harm
when I enjoy full happiness within my soul? Or, how can having
kind hearts around me help me when I do not have God within
me? When God dwells within me, who can harm me? (*Diary*, 455)

Reflection

The suffering will come again. We can't change that. What we can
do, as St. Faustina did, is let peace and happiness not give way to
bitterness. How? By never forgetting that "God dwells within me."

Prayer

Thank You, Kind and Gracious God, for never leaving me and for
always loving me.

Jesus, I trust in You.

August 10

VIRTUE'S CONSTANT COMPANION

> Where there is genuine virtue, there must be
> sacrifice as well;... (*Diary*, 1358)

Reflection

Yes, like building up a muscle, practicing a virtue becomes easier
the more we use it. But, like a muscle, if we don't use it we lose it.
A strong and healthy body, a virtuous and holy soul, demand sacrifice. No shortcuts. No exceptions.

Prayer

Help me choose the better way, Dear Lord. Help me choose virtue
by saying no to what gets in the way of that.

Jesus, I trust in You.

August 11

GOOD FRIENDS

> … [L]ess recollected souls want others to be like them,
> for they [those aware of the presence of God] are a
> constant [source of] remorse to them. (*Diary*, 147)

Reflection

The phrasing in today's quote can be a little tough to follow but it
means this: Some people don't want to be around you if you're a
good person because you remind them that they aren't so good. It's
a sharp contrast. They may criticize at how you live and what you
believe. They'd feel a lot more comfortable if you would only be
more like them. One thing that can help you is spending some time
around like-minded and like-living folks. Time with *good* friends.
None of this about judging or shunning others. It's about giving
yourself a break, and some encouragement.

Prayer

Lord, help me model kindness to those who are unkind to me. Help
my joy attract them to You.

Jesus, I trust in You.

August 12

WHY DOES EVERYONE BOTHER ME TODAY?

I must be on my guard, especially today, because I am becoming over-sensitive to everything. Things I would not pay any attention to when I am healthy bother me today. O my Jesus, my shield and my strength, grant me Your grace that I may emerge victorious from these combats. O my Jesus, transform me into Yourself by the power of Your love, that I may be a worthy tool in proclaiming Your mercy. (*Diary*, 783)

Reflection

It happened to saints. It happens to us. People near to us, and even dear to us, can seem bothersome when we don't feel well or are really tired. Yes, our perception may be off—is probably off—but it's good to know Jesus will help us through that encounter, that morning, that day. Through the power of His love we can nod and find a safe place to retreat until we feel better.

Prayer

Dear Lord, help me be kinder to those who are having a bad day. And, especially, to those who have many bad days, one right after the other.

Jesus, I trust in You.

August 13

SUFFERING: MY CONSTANT COMPANION

> Nothing is as constant as suffering—it always
> faithfully keeps the soul company. (*Diary*, 227)

Reflection

God is more constant than suffering. He's *always* with us. But . . .
suffering does have a way of frequently popping back into our lives
and into our souls. Yes, it too is "faithful" in its visits but, again,
nothing comes near the faithfulness, the eternal consistency, of our
God and of His love for us.

Prayer

Today, Dear Lord, I offer up my sufferings as a prayer for N.

Jesus, I trust in You.

August 14

YOU'RE BEING WATCHED

Today during adoration, the Lord gave me to know
how much He desires a soul to distinguish itself by
deeds of love. And in spirit I saw how many souls are
calling out to us, "Give us God." (*Diary*, 1249)

Reflection

It was the early Christian writer Tertullian who wrote "See how
they love one another," referring to members of the Church. Then,
as now, the followers of Jesus were being watched. You're being
watched, by others and by God. Both want to see your deeds of
love. Your actions that will draw those others to Christ.

Prayer

Dear Lord, let what I do better show my love for You and others.
Jesus, I trust in You.

August 15

PRAY, PRAY, PRAY

I saw the Mother of God unspeakably beautiful. She said to me,
*My daughter, what I demand from you is prayer, prayer, and once again
prayer, for the world especially your country.*

*For nine days receive Holy Communion in atonement and unite yourself
closely to the Holy Sacrifice of the Mass. During these nine days you will
stand before God as an offering; always and everywhere, at all times and
places, day or night, whenever you wake up, pray in the spirit.*

In spirit, one can always remain in prayer. (Diary, 325)

Reflection

There is an urgency from Our Lady. Three times she "*demands*"
us to pray, pray, pray for the world and our country. She asks for
nine days of Holy Communion in atonement. She asks us to unite
ourselves to the Holy Sacrifice of the Mass. It is the highest form of
worship and the highest act of prayer. For peace in our hearts, peace
in our families, and peace in world, let us respond to her call.

Prayer

Queen assumed into Heaven, pray for us and intercede for the dying!
    Jesus, I trust in You.

August 16

CARVING OUT MOMENTS OF SILENCE

The conversations that I hear in this place about worldly matters make me so tired that I nearly faint. (*Diary*, 1788)

Reflection

St. Faustina was talking about life in the convent but the same holds true for us. And, it could be argued, even more so. She never had to deal with a twenty-four-hour news cycle or social (sometimes antisocial) media. Ours is a loud, fast, noisy world, and carving out moments of silence to find slivers of peace takes effort. That's tough to do when *we're* "so tired" we "nearly faint." How wonderful if there could truly be a "universal remote" that let us mute everything except what Our Lord is saying to us and what we want to say to Him. Sometimes silence is more than golden; it's divine. And so worth the effort, no matter how brief the reward.

Prayer

I would appreciate it, Lord, if You and I can share a few quiet moments today.

And tomorrow and every day.

Jesus, I trust in You.

August 17
WHEN TOO MUCH IS TOO MUCH

When I see that the burden is beyond my strength, I
do not consider or analyze it or probe into it, but I run
like a child to the Heart of Jesus and say only one word
to Him: "You can do all things." (*Diary*, 1033)

Reflection

St. Faustina offers practical advice for when we find ourselves in
over our head. No need to try to solve the problem on our own
without first getting someone—Someone—in our corner to help
us. It's not hard to imagine His response: "Of course. I'm so glad you
asked!"

Prayer

Thank You, Dear Jesus, for never abandoning me. Give me the
faith and the wisdom to turn to You—again and again—when I
see that a "burden is beyond my strength." I know it's never beyond
Yours.

Jesus, I trust in You.

August 18

GOD IS NO MICROMANAGER

Jesus gave me to know that even the smallest thing does
not happen on earth without His will. (*Diary*, 1262)

Reflection

St. Faustina is describing what the Church teaches. Yes, He is the
Creator and hasn't abandoned His work. Nor does He control
every move, every choice including all the ones we make. But we
are not without free will. He allows us to choose what we choose.
That freedom is His will for us. Being God, He knows what we will
choose, but we aren't in some way forced to choose it.

Prayer

Thank You, Dear God, for giving me the freedom to choose You
and Your will for me.

Jesus, I trust in You.

August 19

ASK ST. FAUSTINA

A soul arms itself by prayer for all kinds of combat. In whatever state the soul may be, it ought to pray. A soul which is pure and beautiful must pray, or else it will lose its beauty; a soul which is striving after this purity must pray, or else it will never attain it; a soul which is newly converted must pray, or else it will fall again; a sinful soul, plunged in sins, must pray so that it might rise again. There is no soul which is not bound to pray, for every single grace comes to the soul through prayer. (*Diary*, 146)

Reflection

"Do I have to pray, St. Faustina?" "Only if you have a soul, my friend." *"Do I have to be a person of prayer, St. Faustina?"* "Only if your soul is free from sin or mired in sin, my friend."

Prayer

Dear St. Faustina, help me become stronger at being a person of prayer. I want a soul "armed for all kinds of combat."

Jesus, I trust in You.

August 20

NOT OUR CONCERN

The Lord said to me, **It should be of no concern to you how anyone else acts; you are to be My living reflection, through love and mercy.** I answered, "Lord, but they often take advantage of my goodness." **That makes no difference, My daughter. That is no concern of yours. As for you, be always merciful toward other people, and especially toward sinners.** (*Diary*, 1446)

Reflection

We do something really nice for someone, at no small cost or effort on our part, and they don't even say "Thanks." Or worse, they complain about it because it's not enough or *exactly* what they wanted. To which Jesus replies: "That makes no difference, [insert your name here]. That is no concern of yours."

Prayer

Help me to always be merciful toward other people, Lord. Even toward ... well, You know. And help me be a person filled with gratitude. Thank You. (Have I said that lately?)

Jesus, I trust in You.

August 21

WHAT A LIFE!

> I want to live in the spirit of faith. I accept everything
> that comes my way as given me by the loving will of God,
> who sincerely desires my happiness. (*Diary*, 1549)

Reflection

When we imagine the good life we tend to think of wealth, success, health, and freedom from worry. St. Faustina asks for a life led "in the spirit of faith." A life that includes accepting everything God hands her because He's all-good and all-loving. That *does* take faith. And practice.

Prayer

Lord, I want to be happy as You want me to be happy.

Jesus, I trust in You.

August 22

QUEEN MOTHER

A vision of the Mother of God. In the midst of a great brilliance, I saw the Mother of God clothed in a white gown, girt about with a golden cincture; and there were tiny stars, also of gold, over the whole garment, and chevron-shaped sleeves lined with gold. Her cloak was sky-blue, lightly thrown over the shoulders. A transparent veil was delicately drawn over her head, while her flowing hair was set off beautifully by a golden crown which terminated in little crosses. (*Diary*, 1585)

Reflection

On October 11, 1954, Pope Pius XII, in his encyclical *Ad Caeli Reginam*, decreed and instituted the Feast of the Queenship of the Blessed Virgin Mary to be celebrated throughout the world. He decreed that on that day "there be renewed the consecration of the human race to the Immaculate Heart of the Blessed Virgin Mary."

Prayer

O Mary, Virgin Mother of God, we choose you this day to be our Queen, our Advocate, and our Mother. Take us under your protection, and pray for us, dearest Mother, now and at the hour of our death. Amen.

Jesus, I trust in You.

August 23

TAKING PART IN JESUS' DEATH

Oh, what awesome mysteries take place during Mass!
A great mystery is accomplished in the Holy Mass.
With what great devotion should we listen to and
take part in this death of Jesus. (*Diary*, 914)

Reflection

In today's quote St. Faustina is saying what the *Catechism of the Catholic Church* would teach some six decades after her death. One term for the Mass is "the Holy Sacrifice, because it makes present the one sacrifice of Christ the Savior" (130). In St. Faustina's words: "we ... take part in this death of Jesus." They're one and the same. She also uses a contemporary exclamation but not exactly as young people do today. The mysteries of the Mass are ... *awesome!*

Prayer

You *are* awesome, Dear God! I want to take part of the celebration of the Mass with greater devotion.

Jesus, I trust in You.

August 24
A GREAT MYSTERY SOLVED

It is only in eternity that we shall know the great
mystery effected in us by Holy Communion. O most
precious moments of my life! (*Diary*, 840)

Reflection

It isn't just exactly *how* bread can become the Body of Christ that
we don't understand. It's also all the effects of receiving Holy Communion can have on us. Each is a great mystery ... for now. Each
will be answered in the fullness of time. But even now, we can be
certain of this: each will be more proof of God's infinite love for us.

Prayer

O Most Precious Lord of the Eucharist, I love You.

Jesus, I trust in You.

August 25
AT THE FEET OF THE HIDDEN GOD

I spend every free moment at the feet of the hidden God. He is my Master; I ask Him about everything; I speak to Him about everything. Here I obtain strength and light; here I learn everything; here I am given light on how to act toward my neighbor. (*Diary*, 704)

Reflection

In today's quote St. Faustina is talking about her time in adoration before the Blessed Sacrament, "the hidden God." She's telling us that all our time there (or at home in private adoration) doesn't have to be all formal prayers. Like her, we can "speak to Him about everything." And, like her, we can better learn "how to act toward [our] neighbor."

Prayer

Dear Jesus, thank You for letting me speak to You from my heart, and thank You for helping me learn how to better serve You by serving others. Dear Jesus, I adore You.

Jesus, I trust in You.

August 26
IN THE SMALLEST DETAILS

Jesus likes to intervene in the smallest details of our
life, and He often fulfills secret wishes of mine that
I sometimes hide from Him, although I know that
from Him nothing can be hidden. (*Diary*, 360)

Reflection

There's comfort in what St. Faustina says, with what she knows.
God isn't distant. He's right here, with you. God isn't indifferent.
He "likes to intervene in the smallest details" of your life. He knows
you … completely. And loves you, with His "unfathomable" mercy.

Prayer

I'm overwhelmed by Your personal and private love for me, Lord.
  Jesus, I trust in You.

August 27

3+ WORDS

... I would like to say three words to the soul that is determined to strive for sanctity and to derive fruit; that is to say, benefit from confession.

First [word] — complete sincerity and openness.

Second word — humility.

Third word — obedience. (*Diary*, 113)

Reflection

Yes, in the English translation St. Faustina uses six words, not three, but her list is still extremely short and deeply profound. It's a glimpse at how a saint becomes a saint. It doesn't just happen. It takes work. She wanted to be *determined* to *strive* for *sanctity*. And to *derive fruit* from confession. Yes, her sins would be forgiven — as will ours — but she was pushing for spiritual growth by way of confession. She wanted her "personal best" to get better and better. And she knew that took deliberate effort.

Prayer

Dear Lord, help me see the sacrament of confession with new eyes and a deeper appreciation of what it can do to my soul. Help me approach it — help me approach You — with complete sincerity, openness, humility, and obedience.

Jesus, I trust in You.

August 28
A COMPASS CALLED "PRUDENCE"

> Virtue without prudence is not virtue at all. We should often pray to the Holy Spirit for this grace of prudence. Prudence consists in discretion, rational reflection and courageous resolution. (*Diary*, 1106)

Reflection

In today's quote St. Faustina is telling us we can be steeped in a variety of virtues but won't be going anywhere if we don't know how to prudently put each into practice. Or in the words of the *Catechism of the Catholic Church*: "With the help of this virtue we apply moral principles to particular cases without error and overcome doubts about the good to achieve and the evil to avoid" (1806). Prudence tells us "do *this*" and "don't do *that*."

Prayer

Dear Holy Spirit, please give me prudence.

Jesus, I trust in You.

August 29

A GREAT CHANCE

... [W]hen we suffer much we have a great chance to show God that we love Him; ... (*Diary*, 303)

Reflection

If we accept suffering and do something with it. That's what makes the difference. That's what gives it such power. But we don't *have* to. We can choose to. We can get into the habit of choosing to. Every ache and pain, every heartache and hardship, is a "great chance to show God we love Him." To turn that suffering into a prayer *to* Him and pray *for* others.

Prayer

"My Father, if this cannot pass unless I drink it, thy will be done" (Mt 26:42).

Jesus, I trust in You.

August 30

MORE NEED THAN EVER

> O Jesus, make the fount of Your mercy gush forth more abundantly, for humankind is seriously ill and thus has more need than ever of Your compassion. (*Diary*, 793)

Reflection

It seems that in the history of humanity there have been no fully peaceful times, no eras when sin didn't wreak havoc. But there have been moments when peace reigned. There have been people who lived, and loved, and died as they went about doing what God created them to do. As the Church Militant, as the souls on earth, we can add to those moments and places. We can live and love and die as our holy ones have for centuries.

Prayer

Make me a channel of Your peace, Lord. Of Your love. Of Your mercy.

Jesus, I trust in You.

August 31

FILLING THE GAP

Jesus, my Love, today gave me to understand how much He loves me, although there is such an enormous gap between us, the Creator and the creature; and yet, in a way, there is something like equality: love fills up the gap. He Himself descends to me and makes me capable of communing with Him. (*Diary*, 815)

Reflection

Even as St. Faustina was growing in her understanding and appreciation of God's love for her she never lost sight of the foundation of their relationship. One was the Creator, the other the creature. There's an infinite chasm between the two but, at the same time, there isn't. Love fills it. Love connects God and St. Faustina with "something like equality." It's God Himself Who makes it possible for her to commune with her Creator. It's what He does for us, too.

Prayer

Dear Loving Father, forgive me for the times when, by my sins, I widen the gap between us.

Jesus, I trust in You.

CHAPTER NINE

Reflections

FOR

September

September 1

FINDING MY WAY

O holy faith, you are my guidepost! (*Diary*, 763)

Reflection

Maybe if St. Faustina had lived in this century she would have written "O holy faith, you are my GPS." The point is the same: show me the way. Let my faith, let *the* Faith, help me find my way through this world and into life eternal. (Then, too, and sometimes more challenging, at times God asks us to be that "guidepost" for others.)

Prayer

Thank You, Dear Jesus, for not leaving us orphans. Thank You for the Church and for the Holy Spirit who leads it, Who wants to lead me home.

Jesus, I trust in You.

September 2

ONE FOOT ON THE GROUND

In the evening, He gave me to understand how fleeting all earthly things are, and [how] everything that appears great disappears like smoke, and does not give the soul freedom, but weariness. Happy the soul that understands these things and with only one foot touches the earth. (*Diary*, 1141)

Reflection

Yes, we live on the earth and earthly things need to be tended to. Food and shelter, for example, but not exorbitant gourmet meals or a home filled with only the best of the best. In today's quote St. Faustina isn't saying something we haven't all heard a hundred times, but she does use a nice image. One foot necessarily on earth, the other stepping toward heaven.

Prayer

When it comes to earthly possessions, Dear Lord, it's easy to slide from "what I need" to "what I want." Help me remember what I *really* need in this life, and *Who* I really want.

Jesus, I trust in You.

September 3
MOMENTS FOR SILENCE

There are moments when one should be silent, and when it would be inappropriate to talk with creatures; these are the moments when one is dissatisfied with oneself, and when the soul feels as weak as a little child. Then the soul clings to God with all its might. At such times, I live solely by faith, and when I feel strengthened by God's grace, then I am more courageous in speaking and communicating with my neighbors. (*Diary*, 944)

Reflection

In today's quote St. Faustina is saying all of us, saints included, need times when we can step away. Be silent. Think. Reflect. And, in a sense, hold on tight to God. When we can better appreciate, and be comforted by, the faith He's given us. Then, spiritually rested and renewed, we can again step out and be among others.

Prayer

Thank You, Dear Lord, for letting me rest with You and in You.

Jesus, I trust in You.

September 4
THE INNER CALM REMAINS

From the moment when You let me fix the eyes of my
soul on You, O Jesus, I have been at peace.... Sufferings,
adversities, humiliations, failures and suspicions that
have come my way are splinters that keep alive the
fire of my love for You, O Jesus. (*Diary*, 57)

Reflection

We all want that deep sense of peace, one that can't be destroyed
by all the hits we take day after day. In fact, St. Faustina says, they
help us appreciate it more. No matter how many waves furiously
rock the boat, the inner calm remains. Jesus remains. With us. And
we with Him.

Prayer

Give me peace, Dear Lord. Let not my heart be troubled.

Jesus, I trust in You.

September 5
DIFFERENT DAY, DIFFERENT OUTLOOK

The days of my life are not monotonous. When dark clouds cover the sun, like the eagle I will try to brave the billows and make known to others that the sun is not dying out. (*Diary*, 385)

Reflection

Sometimes Faustina writes about her monotonous life but today.... Joy conquers all and confidence takes control. Dark clouds will come, but God is always there.

Prayer

Thank You for joy, Lord. Thank You for confidence. Thank You for moments when I feel Your love and presence so deeply.

Jesus, I trust in You.

September 6
GETTING ALONG

Community life is difficult in itself, but it is doubly difficult
to get along with proud souls. O God, give me a deeper
faith that I may always see in every sister Your holy image
which has been engraved in her soul … (*Diary*, 1522)

Reflection

Family, parish, work, and neighborhood life are each "difficult in
itself." And *at least* "doubly difficult to get along with proud souls."
How is it possible to do that? We need to see in each person God's
"holy image" engraved in their soul. (And, to make it easier for others to get along with us, we need to avoid being a "proud soul.")

Prayer

Today, Dear Lord, I pray especially for those who annoy me most.
Each, made in Your image. Each, Your son or daughter.

Jesus, I trust in You.

September 7

NO CAKEWALK, EVEN FOR A SAINT

In spite of the profound peace my soul is enjoying, I am struggling continuously, and it is often a hard-fought battle for me to walk faithfully along my path; that is, the path which the Lord Jesus wants me to follow. (*Diary*, 1173)

Reflection

After all her talk of peace and doing God's will, St. Faustina confesses the battle continues. There's no strolling along this path. It's step by step, temptation by temptation, grace by grace.

Prayer

Dear Jesus, help me live my "yes" to Your invitation to "Come, follow Me."

Jesus, I trust in You.

September 8

YOU ARE THE HIGHEST HONOR OF OUR RACE

In the evening, when I was praying, the Mother of God told me, *Your lives must be like Mine: quiet and hidden, in unceasing union with God, pleading for humanity and preparing the world for the second coming of God.* (*Diary*, 625)

Reflection

Our Lady cooperated in God's redemptive plan through her yes. And her yes reversed the no of Eve.

Prayer

Dearest Mother, I want to say yes and become an instrument in your hands for the salvation of the world. Help me to cooperate with the Divine Mercy pleading for humanity and rescuing souls. Happy Birthday!

Jesus, I trust in You.

September 9

IN DIFFICULT MOMENTS

Eternal God, in whom mercy is endless and the treasury of compassion inexhaustible, look kindly upon us and increase Your mercy in us, that in difficult moments we might not despair nor become despondent, but with great confidence submit ourselves to Your holy will, which is Love and Mercy itself. (*Diary*, 950)

Reflection

In today's quote St. Faustina is reminding us that even though we may know, on some level, that God's mercy is endless, we still have difficult moments that are challenging. There are times when we lean toward despair and despondency. It's remaining confident in God's mercy—and compassion—and it's submitting ourselves to His holy will that make all the difference in the world. And in the world to come.

Prayer

Dear Heavenly Father, help me find strength in Your mercy, compassion, and will for me.

Jesus, I trust in You.

September 10

THE LASER OF LOVE

I asked Jesus that He deign to light the fire of His love in all souls that were cold. Beneath these rays a heart will grow warm even if it were like a block of ice; even if it were hard as a rock, it will crumble into dust. (*Diary*, 370)

Reflection

St. Faustina died some twenty years before the first laser was built in 1960. But how she describes Jesus' focused and powerful love sure sounds a lot like one. A spiritual one. Indifference and hatred don't stand a chance against it. They "will crumble into dust."

Prayer

Fill me through and through with Your love, Lord, because I want to be through with sin.

Jesus, I trust in You.

September 11

MY FAITHFUL FRIEND

> O Jesus concealed in the Host, my sweet Master and faithful Friend, how happy my soul is to have such a Friend who always keeps me company. I do not feel lonely even though I am in isolation. Jesus-Host, we know each other—that is enough for me. (*Diary*, 877)

Reflection

What a sweet description. Jesus is "my faithful Friend." To you, one person among billions. He's yours. Yes, all others, too, but *yours*. And more than just a friend, He's faithfully your friend. He won't turn on you, won't abandon you, no matter what you do or don't do. Jesus, your faithful Friend, is with you through thick and thin. Truly, the best friend *forever*.

Prayer

Jesus, "my faithful Friend" Who laid down His life for me, help me live for You.

Jesus, I trust in You.

September 12
A NEW LIGHT ON OUR FAULTS

Jesus gave me the grace of knowing myself. In this divine light I see my principal fault; it is pride which takes the form of my closing up within myself and of a lack of simplicity in my relations with Mother Superior [Irene]. The second light concerns speaking. I sometimes talk too much. A thing could be settled in one or two words, and as for me, I take too much time about it. But Jesus wants me to use that time to say some short indulgenced prayers for the souls in purgatory. And the Lord says that every word will be weighed on the day of judgment. (*Diary*, 274)

Reflection

It would be a wonderful, and humbling, thing to truly know ourselves. What would become starkly apparent in that "divine light?" What principal faults would be clearly seen, and what would we want to do to overcome them? To eradicate them? Perhaps they wouldn't be too surprising. And, certainly, they don't have to be in the sharpest focus possible for us to know we have work to do. Important work. Work we can begin today.

Prayer

Dear Lord, help me stop fooling myself about my faults. Help me take them seriously and get to work on getting rid of them.

Jesus, I trust in You.

September 13

TO MY VERY DEPTHS

> I have become interiorly united with God. His presence penetrates me to my very depths and fills me with peace, joy and amazement. After such moments of prayer, I am filled with strength and an extraordinary courage to suffer and struggle. (*Diary*, 480)

Reflection

Yes, at times St. Faustina writes of being weary to the bone physically. We all are. But, in today's quote, she tells us that becoming "interiorly united with God"—that is, closer and closer to Him—our "very depths" can be filled with "peace, joy and amazement." What a wonderful way to live, even when we need more sleep.

Prayer

Lord and Giver of Life, give me strength and courage, and more . . . spiritual pep.

Jesus, I trust in You.

September 14

EARTH'S "GREATEST TREASURE"

> Suffering is the greatest treasure on earth; it purifies the soul.
> In suffering we learn who is our true friend. (*Diary*, 342)

Reflection

Here St. Faustina is using hyperbole (exaggeration for effect), or speaking in a very narrow way. Obviously, the Eucharist is far, far greater than suffering, but suffering is—or can be—a treasure. How? By helping us focus on what really matters, by being offered up as a prayer, and, as St. Faustina points out, by helping us realize who our true Friend is.

Prayer

Lord, help me use my suffering wisely.

We adore You, O Christ, and we praise You, because by Your Holy Cross you have redeemed the world.

Jesus, I trust in You.

September 15

TEARS OF BLOOD

I heard the voice of Our Lady: *Know, My daughter,
that although I was raised to the dignity of Mother of God,
seven swords of pain pierced My heart.* (*Diary*, 786)

Reflection

In the words of Simeon: "a sword will pierce through your own
soul" (Lk 2:35).

Prayer

Hail Mary, full of sorrows, the Crucified is with you; tearful are you
among women, and tearful is the fruit of your womb, Jesus. Holy
Mary, Mother of the Crucified, give tears to us, crucifiers of your
Son, now and at the hour of our death. Amen.

Jesus, I trust in You.

September 16
PRAYING THROUGH THE PAIN

> Let every soul remember these words: "And being
> in anguish, He prayed longer." (*Diary*, 872)

Reflection

Athletes speak of playing through the pain. For St. Faustina, it was "praying" through the pain. What pain? "Torments, dryness, and temptations." No joy. No contentment. At times, seemingly, no hope. Why continue? The same reasons athletes do. To get through it, to overcome it, to move closer to where one wants to be.... Physically for them. Spiritually for her. It's eye-opening to realize, as St. Faustina tells us, that this is what Jesus did during His agony in the garden. It's like part two on His course on "How to Pray." First came what to say: the Our Father. Then it was how to pray, again and again, when what God asks of us seems so frightening, and impossible.

Prayer

Thank You, Dear Jesus, for what You teach me by Your words and by Your example.

Jesus, I trust in You.

September 17

GOD NEVER BLINKS

Oh, how misleading are appearances, and how unjust the judgments. Oh, how often virtue suffers only because it remains silent. To be sincere with those who are incessantly stinging us demands much self-denial. One bleeds, but there are no visible wounds. O Jesus, it is only on the last day that many of these things will be made known. What joy—none of our efforts will be lost! (*Diary*, 236)

Reflection

Yes, God sees everything wrong we do. But, St. Faustina reminds us, He also sees everything *good* we do. Often, those acts are unseen by others. In a sense, until "the last day" they're little secrets the two of you share. And isn't that a happy thought?

Prayer

I want to do good for Your sake, Lord, not for pats on the back from others.

Jesus, I trust in You.

September 18
TRYING THE PATIENCE OF A SAINT

There is a woman here who was once one of our students. Naturally, she puts my patience to the test. She comes to see me several times a day. After each of these visits I am tired out, but I see that the Lord Jesus has sent that soul to me. Let everything glorify You, O Lord. Patience gives glory to God. O how poor the souls are! (*Diary*, 920)

Reflection

Today's quote is a good reminder that saints don't necessarily *have* a lot of patience but — sometimes tested to the edge — they *have to use* whatever amount is theirs. And, of course, the same is true for us.

Prayer

I realize, Lord, that You may have given me all the patience I need. I need your help in using it better.

Jesus, I trust in You.

September 19

GRACE IN THIS HOUR

O life so dull and monotonous, how many treasures you contain!
When I look at everything with the eyes of faith, no two hours
are alike, and the dullness and monotony disappear. The grace
which is given me in this hour will not be repeated in the next.
It may be given me again, but it will not be the same grace.
Time goes on, never to return again. Whatever is enclosed in it
will never change; it seals with a seal for eternity. (*Diary*, 62)

Reflection

"Dull and monotonous." Plod, plod, plod. Except … it isn't either
of those when we "look at everything with the eyes of faith." God
is giving us particular graces for this year, this month, this day. For
this *hour*. Each a gift like no other because no hour is exactly like
another. It's grace *in* this hour *for* this hour.

Prayer

Thank You, Dear Generous Lord, for giving me the grace I need for
every step I take on my journey home to You.

Jesus, I trust in You.

September 20
INSPIRED TO PRAY

Oh, dying souls are in such great need of prayer! O Jesus, inspire souls to pray often for the dying. (*Diary*, 1015)

Reflection

In today's quote St. Faustina is giving us two pieces of advice. First, reminding us that those who are dying greatly need our prayers. And second, asking Jesus to touch our heart so that we increase those prayers. With a little effort, we can make that a habit with eternal consequences, eternal blessings.

Prayer

Father, Son, and Holy Spirit, I ask that those who are dying be blessed with Your love, mercy, and peace. Welcome them home to You.

Jesus, I trust in You.

September 21

THE SHIELD OF MERCY

O Jesus, shield me with Your mercy and also
judge me leniently ... (*Diary*, 1093)

Reflection

We tend to think of a shield as something made of iron or steel.
Or, in science fiction, some sort of force field. But a shield made
of mercy? How would that work? Very well, thanks be to God,
the source of that mercy. What would our life, and our upcoming
judgment, be without it? We wouldn't stand a chance. Same, too,
without the leniency of our judge. We don't deserve heaven, we
don't earn heaven, we—despite all that we do and fail to do—are
handed the promise of heaven, with the choice to accept it or not.

Prayer

Christ, as a shield, overshadow me.

Jesus, I trust in You.

September 22

"GOD-MADE," NOT "SELF-MADE"

> Let no one trust too much in his own self. (*Diary*, 1495)

Reflection

No one achieves success in any way without some assistance from others. God created us to help and need help. To rely too much on ourselves alone is to be leaning on a fool. To put all our trust in ... us ... is to ignore our Creator and all He has to give us.

Prayer

Help me have more faith in You, Lord, so that I have the right kind of faith in me.

Jesus, I trust in You.

September 23

A "HEAVENLY" BREAK

> I must not let myself become absorbed in the whirl of work,
> [but] take a break to look up to heaven. (*Diary*, 226)

Reflection

"Whirl of work." What a great translation from the original Polish edition of the *Diary*.

What an image that's so easy for all of us to imagine because … we've been there more than a time or two. And St. Faustina's advice? Go get another cup of coffee? Head for the candy machine? Simply look up to heaven. Take a deep breath and have a little "prayer break."

Prayer

When work is getting me down, Dear Lord, remind me to look up … to You.

Jesus, I trust in You.

September 24

THE GIFTS AT MASS

> One day we will know what God is doing for us in each Mass, and what sort of gift He is preparing in it for us. (*Diary*, 914)

Reflection

"Bringing up the gifts" is a common expression these days for presenting the wine and hosts to the Mass' celebrant at the beginning of the Offertory. And, yes, we're called to "offer" ourselves, too. St. Faustina is reminding us this isn't a one-sided arrangement. Far, far, from it. Our generous God lavishes us with more than we can ever imagine.

Prayer

Dear Lord, at Mass You give me gift upon gift upon gift. You're so kind to me, so good to me, so loving.

Jesus, I trust in You.

September 25
LOOKING LIKE OUR FATHER

We resemble God most when we forgive our neighbors.
God is Love, Goodness, and Mercy. (*Diary*, 1148)

Reflection

It's no secret that advertisements feature extremely good-looking people. The message? Buy this, use this, drink this. Today St. Faustina does a little marketing of her own. Want to be more like God? Forgive those who have wronged you.

Prayer

Beloved Jesus, help me be quicker to say, "I forgive you." Even seventy time seven times. (Which I know means an infinite number and isn't limited to 490.)

Jesus, I trust in You.

September 26

WORN OUT

I suffer great pain at the sight of the sufferings of others. All these sufferings are reflected in my heart. I carry their torments in my heart so that it even wears me out physically. I would like all pains to fall upon me so as to bring relief to my neighbor. (*Diary*, 1039)

Reflection

One of the costs of loving is suffering. Those nearest and dearest to our hearts are also the ones that can break them. Yes, sometimes by what they do, intentionally or unintentionally. But also sometimes by what happens to them. A job loss. A serious illness or condition. And, of course, their death. Like St. Faustina, we can say "all these sufferings are reflected in my heart." And we, too, become worn out physically. Emotionally. Mentally. And spiritually. This is when Jesus can speak to us. When, through His words in Scripture, He softly, tenderly says to us, "Come to me, all who labor and are heavy laden, and I will give you rest" (Mt 11:28).

Prayer

Give me rest, Lord. Give me peace. Give me Yourself.

Jesus, I trust in You.

September 27
AN ANSWER TO THEIR PRAYERS

Almost all night I had such violent pains that it seemed all my intestines were torn to pieces.... Jesus demanded suffering, but not death. O my Jesus, do with me as You please. Only give me strength to suffer. Since Your strength supports me, I shall bear everything. (*Diary*, 1613)

Reflection

"Lord, stop my suffering" and "Lord, give me the strength to suffer" are similar but different prayers. He can do either and will always choose what's best for us. Sometimes the deepest act of faith is accepting God's choice, God's will, God's plan.

Prayer

Dear Lord, help me help those who are suffering. Help me remember that, on some days, You send *me* as Your answer to their prayers.

Jesus, I trust in You.

September 28

MORE THAN A SECOND CHANCE

As I was meditating on the sin of the Angels and their immediate punishment, I asked Jesus why the Angels had been punished as soon as they had sinned. I heard a voice: **Because of their profound knowledge of God. No person on earth, even though a great saint, has such knowledge of God as an Angel has.** (*Diary*, 1332)

Reflection

In today's quote St. Faustina addresses two questions a lot of us have had. Why didn't the fallen angels get even a second chance? And why does God give us so many throughout our time on earth? We simply don't have the "profound knowledge of God" that they do. But what we do know is this: God sent His Son, Who was crucified for us. Such is His love and mercy.

Prayer

Thank You, Dear God, for the infinite mercy You offer to me and to my loved ones. That You offer to all.

Jesus, I trust in You.

September 29

THE PRESENCE, AND PRESENTS, OF ANGELS

On the Feast of Saint Michael the Archangel, I saw by my side that great Leader, who spoke these words to me: "The Lord has ordered me to take special care of you. Know that you are hated by evil; but do not fear—'Who is like God!'" And he disappeared. But I feel his presence and assistance. (*Diary*, 706)

Reflection

What amazing defenders and guardians God has given us! Michael, whose name means "who is like God." Gabriel, whose name means "strength of God." And Raphael, whose name means "healing power of God." Each a reflection of their Creator, just as we're called to be.

Prayer

St. Michael, St. Gabriel, and St. Raphael, be with me now and with those I love.

Jesus, I trust in You.

September 30
TAKING TIME TO REFLECT

I was reflecting on how much God had suffered and on how great was the love He had shown for us, and on the fact that we still do not believe that God loves us so much. O Jesus, who can understand this? What suffering it is for our Savior! How can He convince us of His love if even His death cannot convince us? I called upon the whole of heaven to join me in making amends to the Lord for the ingratitude of certain souls. (*Diary*, 319)

Reflection

It's encouraging that we can do what St. Faustina did: reflect. And we can reach the conclusion she reached: this is beyond me, God. Today she asks what else could Jesus do to prove His love for us that He hasn't already done. He died for us, and that's enough!

Prayer

Eternal Father, help me remember that Your Dearly Beloved Son offered up His Body and Blood, Soul and Divinity for me.

Jesus, I trust in You.

CHAPTER TEN

Reflections
FOR
October

October 1

A GREAT SAINT

"But, little Therese, shall I be a saint as you are, raised to the altar?" And she answered, "Yes, you will be a saint just as I am...." (*Diary*, 150)

Let no soul, even the most miserable, fall prey to doubt; for, as long as one is alive, each one can become a great saint, so great is the power of God's grace. It remains only for us not to oppose God's action. (*Diary*, 283)

Reflection

Bad news in today's quote. Each one of us can become a saint. *You* can become a saint. Why's that bad to hear? Because it blows apart the excuses we make to ourselves and to God. "Worse" yet, notice St. Faustina didn't just say "a saint" but "a *great* saint." There's work to be done.

Prayer

Holy Spirit, Lord and Giver of Life, help me conform my actions to Yours. Help me do what You created me to do in order to become what You created me to become.

Jesus, I trust in You.

October 2

FEAST OF THE HOLY GUARDIAN ANGELS

SUCH A GUEST AND WITNESS

I thanked God for His goodness, that He gives us angels for companions. Oh, how little people reflect on the fact that they always have beside them such a guest, and at the same time a witness to everything! Remember, sinners, that you likewise have a witness to all your deeds. (*Diary*, 630)

Reflection

St. Faustina is telling us that angels—and in particular our guardian angel—provide two things. First, a traveling partner on our journey to get us home to heaven. And second, someone who, without being intrusive, helps us stay accountable for what we're doing. Helps us see our actions, or inaction, through angelic eyes ... and through the eyes of God.

Prayer

Thank you for being with me through thick and thin, dear guardian angel. Help me choose what's right and pleasing to God.

Jesus, I trust in You.

October 3

WORDS FOR US, TOO

I do not want to write much about external matters, for they are not the reason for my writing; I want in particular to note the graces granted me by the Lord, because these are not only for me, but for many other souls as well. (*Diary*, 710)

Reflection

Today St. Faustina tells us she's writing—her long and often theologically deep—*Diary* "for many other souls as well." That's us. That's *you*. No, mostly likely we won't receive the particular graces granted to her. (The visions!) But we can know this with certainty: just as He did with St. Faustina, Our Lord stands ready to enter our mind, our heart, and our soul in ways that are just right for us. That are perfect for you.

Prayer

Thank You, Dear Lord, for the particular graces You've given me. For the many blessings I've received, and that are yet to come.

Jesus, I trust in You.

October 4

GOING TO ST. FAUSTINA

Today, one of the sisters ... came to see me and said, "Sister, I have a strange feeling, as though something were telling me to come to you and commend to you certain problems of mine before you die, and that perhaps you will be able to beseech the Lord Jesus and arrange these things for me. Something keeps telling me that you will be able to obtain this for me." I answered her with equal frankness that, yes, I felt in my soul that after my death I would be able to obtain more from the Lord Jesus than at the present time. "I will remember you, Sister, before His throne." (*Diary*, 1614)

Reflection

Like the sister in today's quote we can go to St. Faustina ... now. She stands ready to remember *us* "before His throne."

Prayer

Dear St. Faustina, please intercede for me. I need help with

_____.

Jesus, I trust in You.

October 5

AS MY DEATH DRAWS NEARER

I do not know, O Lord, at what hour You will come
And so I keep constant watch and listen …
I wait for You, Lord, in calm and silence,
With great longing in my heart.…
Come then, at last, my most sweet Lord
And take my thirsting heart
There, to Your home in the lofty regions of heaven.… (*Diary*, 1589)

Reflection

St. Faustina died five weeks after her thirty-third birthday and she knew the end was coming. She had been battling poor health for more than a year and it was only a matter of time. And for her, as for many who must live that final time with a terminal illness, it couldn't come soon enough. Yes, on God's schedule but, awaited with "with great longing." Eager to go home.

Prayer

Dear Lord, be with all those who are terminally ill, especially for those who are afraid because they don't know You. And … for those who are afraid even though they do know You.

Jesus, I trust in You.

October 6
STEALING GOD'S GLORY

On several occasions, I have learned how some religious
defend their own glory under the pretext of being concerned
for the glory of God, whereas it is not a question of the glory
of God, but of glory of self. O Jesus, how painful this has been
for me! What secrets the day of Your judgment will bring
to light! How can one steal God's gifts? (*Diary*, 1149)

Reflection

Yes, "all for the glory of God" but—some people seem to believe—can't the one doing whatever it is take a little cut off the
top? A little "Look at me! Look what *I* did!" It's clear that really
bothered St. Faustina and wasn't all that rare in the convent. So,
too, with our life in a family, parish, or workplace. In the convent
or in our community, standing up (unbidden) to take a bow doesn't
square with "meek and humble of heart."

Prayer

Lord, keep me seated and quiet when I'm tempted to stand, take a
bow, and say, "Look at me and what I did!"

Jesus, I trust in You.

October 7

THE KEY TO HAPPINESS

In the evening, when I was walking in the garden saying my rosary and came to the cemetery, I opened the gate a little and began to pray for a while, and I asked them interiorly, "You are very happy are you not?" Then I heard the words, "We are happy in the measure that we have fulfilled God's will"—and then silence as before. I became introspective and reflected for a long time on how I am fulfilling God's will and how I am profiting from the time that God has given me. (*Diary*, 515)

Reflection

There it is: the key to temporal and eternal happiness. Do God's will.

Prayer

Today, Lord, I offer my rosary for the holy souls in purgatory, now in union with Your will. Have mercy on them, Dear Lord. Let them rest in peace ... face-to-face with You.

Jesus, I trust in You.

October 8

PATIENCE AND PRAYER

During meditation, the sister on the kneeler next to mine keeps coughing and clearing her throat, sometimes without a break. It occurred to me once that I might take another place for the time of the meditation, because Mass had already been offered. But then I thought that if I did change my place, the sister would notice this and might feel hurt that I had moved away from her. So I decided to continue in prayer in my usual place, and to offer this act of patience to God. Toward the end of the meditation, my soul was flooded with God's consolation, and this to the limit of what my heart could bear; and the Lord gave me to know that if I had moved away from that sister I would have moved away also from those graces that flowed into my soul. (*Diary*, 1311)

Reflection

We have something we really want or need to do and someone near to us is.... Oh, there are so many things they can unknowingly do to distract and irritate us. That can be when we're called upon to perform our own "act of patience," which is so seldom easy.

Prayer

Give me more, Lord, of that wonderful (and hard-earned) virtue of patience. Not just for my sake, but the sake of others around me.

Jesus, I trust in You.

October 9

ABANDONING ONESELF

O my Jesus, You have tested me so many times in this
short life of mine! I have come to understand so many
things, and even such that now amaze me. Oh, how
good it is to abandon oneself totally to God and to give
Him full freedom to act in one's soul! (*Diary*, 134)

Reflection

No matter the length of our time on earth, again and again — as
with St. Faustina — God "tests" us. He challenges us. He teaches us.
He allows us to, step by step, move closer to becoming the son or
daughter He created us to be. To use our free will to answer yes to
what He asks.

Prayer

God gives us Our Lady to help us abandon our will to God. Ask for
her intercession.

Mary, I renounce my spirit, and I ask for your spirit.

Mary, take away my thoughts and give me your thoughts.

Mary, take away my desires and give me your desires.

Mary, take away my feelings and give me your feelings.

I am totally yours and everything I have I offer You. O my beloved
Jesus, through Mary Your Most Holy Mother.

Jesus, I trust in You.

October 10

EVIL IS LIMITED

Praise the Lord, my soul, for everything, and glorify His mercy, for His goodness is without end. Everything will pass, but His mercy is without limit or end. And although evil will attain its measure, in mercy there is no measure. (*Diary*, 423)

Reflection

Just as Christ conquered sin and death, His mercy conquered evil. Sin, death, and evil are limited. Yes, the evil in our world is huge, but Divine Mercy is infinite … and eternal.

Prayer

God of Mercy and Love, help me say no to sin and evil. May my death be the doorway that leads to eternal life with You.

Jesus, I trust in You.

October 11

NEITHER DEATH NOR HEALTH

I wish to speak of one more thing that I have experienced: when God gives neither death nor health, and [when] this lasts for many years, people become accustomed to this and consider the person as not being ill. Then there begins a whole series of silent sufferings. Only God knows how many sacrifices the soul makes. (*Diary*, 1509)

Reflection

"Make me better, Lord, or take me now." It's not an uncommon prayer for those who have greatly suffered for a long time but still, for some unknown reason, have not been called home to heaven. They're experiencing "a whole series of silent suffering" that we who are healthy, we who have much to live for, know little or nothing about. What we *do* know is they need our ongoing prayers and, if appropriate, our presence in their life.

Prayer

Dear Lord, bring comfort to those who are silent sufferers.

Jesus, I trust in You.

October 12

FLAME OF LOVE

My spirit delights and feeds more and more on Your wisdom, which I am getting to know more and more deeply. And in this, the vastness of Your mercy becomes more and more manifest to me. O my Jesus, the effect of all this knowledge on my soul is that I am being transformed into a flame of love towards You, my God. (*Diary*, 1456)

Reflection

What a lovely image. What a lovely sharing. St. Faustina's spirit is "delighted." She "feeds more and more" on God's wisdom which she's getting "to know more and more deeply." Words of a young woman in love. The type of love, the type of transformation, Jesus offers all of us if we, too, spend more time simply getting to know Him.

Prayer

I want to learn more about You, Dear Jesus, day by day. I want to fall deeper in love with You, who are so deeply in love with me.

Jesus, I trust in You.

October 13

A PRAYER FOR PRIESTS

> O Jesus, give us fervent and holy priests! Oh, how great is the dignity of the priest, but at the same time, how great is his responsibility! Much has been given you, O priest, but much will also be demanded of you ... (*Diary*, 941)

Reflection

There's never been an easy time for priests and ours is no exception. Now, as always, priests need our prayers and our support.

Prayer

Great High Priest, thank You for the good and holy men You've chosen for the priesthood to serve You by serving us. Richly bless them for their many sacrifices.

Jesus, I trust in You.

October 14

One day, one of the Mothers [probably Mother Jane] poured out so much of her anger on me and humiliated me so much that I thought I would not be able to endure it. She said to me, "You queer, hysterical visionary, get out of this room; go on with you, Sister!" She continued to pour out upon my head everything she could think of.... Satan always takes advantage of such moments; thoughts of discouragement began to rise to the surface — for your faithfulness and sincerity — this is your reward. How can one be sincere when one is so misunderstood?... Suddenly I heard a voice within my soul, **Do not fear; I am with you.** And an unusual light illumined my mind, and I understood that I should not give in to such sorrows. (*Diary*, 128–129)

Reflection

Mother Jane didn't mince words. She attacked St. Faustina. One that left the "hysterical visionary" shattered in so many ways but not enough to fail to notice.... When we fall to pieces like that it can be easier for Satan to slip in and plant seeds of doubt and mistrust. Then, and always, God is telling us, "Do not fear. I am with you."

Prayer

Dear Lord, I forgive all those who have "attacked" me.
     Jesus, I trust in You.

October 15

COMMUNITY LIFE — WHAT A MYSTERY!

O my Jesus, You know how difficult community life is, how many misunderstandings and misconceptions, despite at times the most sincere good will on both sides. But that is Your mystery, O Lord. We shall know it in eternity; however, our judgments should always be mild. (*Diary*, 720)

Reflection

One has to wonder what a vocations director would think of St. Faustina's words about life in a religious community: "many misunderstandings and misconceptions." Still, that can also describe life in a family, parish, neighborhood, and workplace. It describes life on earth. St. Faustina's advice? "Our judgments should always be mild." Or, put in a modern way: "be cool."

Prayer

Help me be cool, Dear St. Faustina, when someone around me is really making me hot under the collar.

Jesus, I trust in You.

October 16

TIP FROM AN ANGEL

> When I went to the garden one afternoon, my Guardian Angel said to me, "Pray for the dying." And so I began at once to pray the rosary with the gardeners for the dying. After the rosary, we said various prayers for the dying. (*Diary*, 314)

Reflection

It's encouraging to see that from time to time St. Faustina needed a little reminder. In this quote, the suggestion comes from her guardian angel: "Pray for the dying." But, of course, St. Faustina takes it one step further, getting others involved. We can do the same. Out on a walk by ourselves, for example, we can pray privately. At Mass, with others, when the requests during the Prayers of the Faithful are opened to members of the congregation. Yes, it's *memento mori* but, here, not "remember *you're going* to die." It's "remember *others who are* dying."

Prayer

St. Joseph, foster father of Jesus Christ and true spouse of the Blessed Virgin Mary, pray for us and for the dying of this day and night.

Jesus, I trust in You.

October 17

NO FAIRY TALE

I saw that my suffering and prayer shackled Satan and snatched many souls from his clutches. (*Diary*, 1465)

Reflection

What an image. *Shackling* ... and *snatching* ... from his *clutches*. It sounds like a fairy tale except, of course, it's true. It's *you* who can snap on the shackles and snatch others from ... Satan. He's no fairy-tale character. Frightening, yes. Invincible, no. It's you who has the power — by offering up your suffering and prayers — to help save countless souls.

Prayer

St. Michael the Archangel, defend me in battle, and by my suffering and prayers, help me defend others.

Jesus, I trust in You.

October 18

THIS SEAT RESERVED

... [M]y Guardian Angel beckoned me to be silent, and I came before the throne of God. I saw a great and inaccessible light, and I saw a place destined for me, close to God. But what it was like I do not know, because a cloud covered it. However, my Guardian Angel said to me, "Here is your throne, for your faithfulness in fulfilling the will of God." (*Diary*, 683)

Reflection

Again and again and again, St. Faustina is told how important it is to do the will of God. And, in passage after passage, she teaches us what a huge difference that makes in our life on earth and in heaven. Our own reserved seat, our own "throne," is waiting for us there. But like the guests in the Parable of the Wedding Banquet (see Mt 22:1–14), we need proper attire. We need to "cloak ourselves" in doing God's will.

Prayer

Dear Heavenly Father, help me better realize and appreciate how doing *Your* will is *my* way to life eternal with You.

Jesus, I trust in You.

October 19
THE MEANING OF SUCCESS

O my Jesus, You do not give a reward for the successful performance of a work, but for the good will and the labor undertaken. Therefore, I am completely at peace, even if all my undertakings and efforts should be thwarted or should come to naught. If I do all that is in my power, the rest is not my business. And therefore the greatest storms do not disturb the depths of my peace; the will of God dwells in my conscience. (*Diary*, 952)

Reflection

We tend to assume that if we sincerely undertake something for God it's going to end in a rousing success. But that doesn't always happen. St. Faustina explains why: our definition of "success" isn't the same as God's. What He asks is for us to work *toward* this not *achieve* this. Why? The Lord doesn't always explain his reasons. Our job is to work.

Prayer

Give me the faith, Dear Lord, to do what You're asking me to do. Even when Your goal for me isn't what I expected.

Jesus, I trust in You.

October 20

WHAT'S MY MISSION?

O my God, I am conscious of my mission in the Holy Church. It is my constant endeavor to plead for mercy for the world. (*Diary*, 482)

Reflection

St. Faustina had hers. You have yours. *Your* mission in the Holy Church. A work to accomplish. You are the only one in the world that can fulfill it. No one else has your mission.

How to know it, how to fulfill it? Prayer. By staying close to, by relying on, the One Who has chosen you, Who has called you, Who is with you every step, every misstep, and every setback along your way. Along His way for you.

Prayer

Speak, Lord. Your servant is trying hard to listen.

Jesus, I trust in You.

October 21

THE ENVY OF ANGELS

If the angels were capable of envy, they would envy us
for two things; one is the receiving of Holy Communion,
and the other is suffering. (*Diary*, 1804)

Reflection

This is such a lovely, and startling, thought. We have what angels
don't. God giving himself to us in the Eucharist, and His allowing
us to join our suffering to His for the help of souls on earth and in
purgatory. Like the angels in Scripture, we're called and we're sent.

Prayer

Angel of God, my guardian dear, thank you for being at my side as
I receive Our Lord in Holy Communion, and as I join my sufferings
to His sufferings on Calvary.

Jesus, I trust in You.

October 22

CHRIST'S "CONDUIT"

I want to be completely transformed into Your mercy and
to be Your living reflection, O Lord. May the greatest of all
divine attributes, that of Your unfathomable mercy, pass
through my heart and soul to my neighbor. (*Diary*, 163)

Reflection

It's a wonderful image. Christ's mercy passing through our heart
and soul to reach a neighbor. But, it's not like we're just some sort
of pipeline. How can His mercy move through us to others? By *our*
being merciful. Just as we have the duty and privilege of helping others experience God's love by our loving them, so too with
mercy. Again, it's not by our preaching but by our actions and their
coming to understand why we do what we do.

Prayer

To borrow and adapt a line from St. Francis of Assisi: Make me a
channel of Your mercy.

Jesus, I trust in You.

October 23
READY FOR BATTLE ... AND PRAYER

Let the soul be aware that, in order to pray and persevere in prayer, one must arm oneself with patience and cope bravely with exterior and interior difficulties. The interior difficulties are discouragement, dryness, heaviness of spirit and temptations. The exterior difficulties are human respect and time; one must observe the time set apart for prayer. (*Diary*, 147)

Reflection

Who would have guessed finding spiritual peace meant arming for spiritual war? St. Faustina lays it out for us. Here, in terms we can easily understand, is not only how to pray, but how to persevere in praying.

Prayer

Help me gear up, Lord. Help me fight the difficulties on every front to win the victory of drawing closer to You.

Jesus, I trust in You.

October 24

COUNTING ON THE SHEPHERD,
NOT COUNTING SHEEP

Now that I have difficulty sleeping at night, because my suffering won't allow it, I visit all the churches and chapels and, if only for a brief moment, I make an act of adoration before the Blessed Sacrament. (*Diary*, 1501)

Reflection

Probably most of us have a favorite method of finally dropping off to sleep when we need it. For St. Faustina, it wasn't counting sheep but "visiting" the Shepherd. How? What's she describes is "spiritual adoration." Unable to come before Our Lord in the convent chapel, she "visited" Him in nearby churches and chapels. We can do the same. (And not just when we can't sleep.) No, not bilocate—be in two places at one time—but spiritually return to ... the church of our youth or young adulthood. A basilica we remember from a vacation. Our own parish or a nearby Eucharistic chapel.

Prayer

Dear Lord in the Blessed Sacrament, I adore You.
Jesus, I trust in You.

October 25
PILING ON

Let us beware of adding to the suffering of others, because that is displeasing to the Lord.... This is a grave and common defect in religious life; namely, that when one sees a suffering soul, one always wants to add even more suffering. I do not say that everyone acts like this, but there are some. We take the liberty of passing all sorts of judgments, and we repeat them when we would do better to remain silent. (*Diary*, 117)

Reflection

In football, it's called "piling on" and comes with a fifteen-yard penalty. That's when a player is already down on the ground and someone from the opposing team deliberately crashes on top of him. In a convent it's ... "a grave and common defect." Out in the world ... well, you know. St. Faustina is warning us that, in or out of the convent, it comes with a spiritual penalty much more severe than fifteen yards on a ball field.

Prayer

Oh, Dear Lord, sometimes it's so easy and so satisfying to pick on someone who can't put up any kind of a defense. Forgive me for adding more suffering to an already suffering soul. If it can be done, help me also go and ask his or her forgiveness.

Jesus, I trust in You.

October 26

WHERE CREDIT IS DUE

O Jesus, my Love, You know that it has only been for a short while that I have acted toward my neighbor guided solely by Your love. You alone know of my efforts to do this. It comes to me more easily now, but if You Yourself did not kindle that love in my soul, I would not be able to persevere in this. This is due to Your Eucharistic love which daily sets me afire. (*Diary*, 1769)

Reflection

In today's quote St. Faustina isn't asking for some kind of plaque or bonus for the good job she's been doing loving her neighbor. Not even a saint could keep up that kind of behavior without God's help. Or, more specifically, "Your Eucharistic love which daily sets me afire." Same Lord, same Eucharist, same relationship offered to us. Ready, willing, and able to fire *us* up. Every day.

Prayer

Thank You, Lord, for paying such close and loving attention to each of us. To me. I want to be guided by Your love. I want You to be the foundation of how I act toward my neighbors. And I know You want that, too.

Jesus, I trust in You.

October 27

A SNARE OF WORDS

O my Jesus, when someone is unkind and unpleasant toward us, it is difficult enough to bear this kind of suffering. But this is very little in comparison to a suffering which I cannot bear; namely, that which I experience when someone exhibits kindness towards me and then lays snares at my feet at every step I take. What great will power is necessary to love such a soul for God's sake.

Many a time one has to be heroic in loving such a soul as God demands. If contact with that person were infrequent, it would be easier to endure, but when one lives in close contact with the person and experiences this at each step, this demands a very great effort. (*Diary*, 1241)

Reflection

St. Faustina didn't pull any punches. She bluntly told Jesus that being around those who said mean and ugly things about her behind her back "demands a very great effort." We all have opportunities "to be heroic in loving such a soul as God demands." And, through His grace, we can choose to do that.

Prayer

Forgive me, Heavenly Father, for the times my words have hurt others. Help me better love those whose words have hurt me.

Jesus, I trust in You.

October 28

PREPARED FOR WHAT'S HARD TO BEAR

> ... I then answered immediately, "Jesus, I accept everything that You wish to send me; I trust in Your goodness." At that moment, I felt that by this act I glorified God greatly. But I armed myself with patience. As soon as I left the chapel, I had an encounter with reality. I do not want to describe the details, but there was as much of it as I was able to bear. I would not have been able to bear even one drop more. (*Diary*, 190)

Reflection

We've all experienced it. After a time of prayer, a Mass, a visit to the Blessed Sacrament, a retreat, we're hit in the face with ... "reality," to use St. Faustina's term. With all the day-to-day people and problems—including the people who give us problems. We'd be wise to "arm" ourselves with patience. To stock up when we can. To be prepared, and so not caught off guard, when life can be so *irritating*.

Prayer

Arm me with patience, Dear Lord. Be at my side when "reality" comes rushing in.

Jesus, I trust in You.

October 29

FLYING BLIND

I have great reverence for St. Michael the Archangel; he had no example to follow in doing the will of God, and yet he fulfilled God's will faithfully. (*Diary*, 667)

Reflection

We have so many angels and good souls we can learn from and imitate. Not so for St. Michael. In that sense, he was ... flying blind. Now, just as he and the others can be examples for us, God asks us to be examples for those around us in our own lives. Part of our vocation is to demonstrate what it means to faithfully fulfill God's will for us.

Prayer

All you angels and saints, pray for me! And thank you.

Jesus, I trust in You.

October 30
PREPARING FOR DEATH

In the meditation on death, I prepared myself as if for real death. I examined my conscience and searched all my affairs at the approach of death and, thanks be to grace, my affairs were directed toward that ultimate goal. This filled my heart with great gratitude to God, and I resolved to serve my God even more faithfully in the future. One thing alone is necessary: to put my old self to death and to begin a new life. In the morning, I prepared to receive Holy Communion as if it were to be the last in my life, and after Holy Communion I brought before my imagination my actual death, and I said the prayers for the dying and then the *De Profundis* for my own soul. (*Diary*, 1343)

Reflection

Less than a year before St. Faustina's death, her words, her example, are good ones for us. How can we, here and now, "put our old self to death and begin a new life"? How often do we consider our own death? How often do we pray for the dying?

Prayer

Dear Lord and Beloved Blessed Mother, help me be prepared for my death. To die a happy death — in the state of grace. Help me die to myself now so I can live with both of you forever.

Jesus, I trust in You.

October 31

BIG LOVE, BIG POWER

> When God loves, He loves with all His Being, with all
> the power of His Being. If God has loved me in this way,
> how should I respond—I, His spouse? (*Diary*, 392)

Reflection

It's obvious that there was one idea that stuck in St. Faustina's
mind: God *really* loves us. Not the way we love God or love each
other, but as only He can love us. With all His Being, with all the
power of His Being. And how should we respond—we, His son or
daughter?

Prayer

I'm too small, Dear God, too finite, too sinful, to love You as You
should be loved. Help me do that the best I can today. And a little
better tomorrow.

Jesus, I trust in You.

CHAPTER ELEVEN

Reflections
FOR
November

November 1

ALL SAINTS DAY

A PRAYER TO THE SAINTS

Help me, happy inhabitants of the heavenly homeland, so that your sister may not falter on the way. Although the desert is fearful, I walk with lifted head and eyes fixed on the sun; that is to say, on the merciful Heart of Jesus. (*Diary*, 886)

Reflection

What a lovely description (and use of alliteration): "happy inhabitants of the heavenly homeland." The souls in heaven, some canonized by the Church, many more (including our loved ones) not, but still there. Both types ready to help us, encourage us, console us. To be with us as we "walk with lifted head and eyes fixed on" ... the Son.

Prayer

Thank you, Dear Souls in Heaven, for all you do for me. Help me live my life as you lived yours.

Jesus, I trust in You.

November 2

PRAYERS FROM THE HEART FOR THE SOULS

> Jesus, I plead with You for the souls that are most in need of prayer. I plead for the dying; be merciful to them. I also beg You, Jesus, to free all souls from purgatory. (*Diary*, 240)

Reflection

Faustina offers three prayers from the heart for souls. Little prayers, huge requests. We don't have to "find the right words." We just have to tell God what's weighing heavy on our heart.

Prayer

Today, Dear Jesus, I plead, I beg, for N.

Jesus, I trust in You.

November 3

MY BIG HEART

O Jesus, my love extends beyond the world, to the souls suffering in purgatory, and I want to exercise mercy toward them by means of indulgenced prayers. (*Diary*, 692)

Reflection

It seems St. Faustina adopted and modified the motivational suggestion to "Go big!" Hers is "Pray big!" Pray for all the souls living on earth and all those in purgatory in one sincere and humble prayer. Why not? God's mercy is ... beyond huge. And she has a suggestion, too. Take advantage of "indulgenced prayers." (*See the Appendix for more about indulgences.*)

Prayer

Heavenly Father, help me love big, serve others big, and do Your will big.

Jesus, I trust in You.

November 4

A SPIRITUAL STOREHOUSE

O Savior of the world. I unite myself with Your mercy. My Jesus, I join all my sufferings to Yours and deposit them in the treasury of the Church for the benefit of souls. (*Diary*, 740)

Reflection

Not only do we benefit from the "treasury of the Church" but, as St. Faustina shows by her example, we can add to it. What is it? The superabundant merits of Christ and the saints. The Church draws from it to confer spiritual benefits, such as indulgences, on us. Very simply put, it's a spiritual storehouse designed to give us the help we need.

Prayer

Accept my suffering, Dear Savior of the world, for the benefit of souls.

Jesus, I trust in You.

November 5

PURGATORY: SOULS LONGING FOR GOD

I saw my Guardian Angel, who ordered me to follow him. In a moment I was in a misty place full of fire in which there was a great crowd of suffering souls. They were praying fervently, but to no avail, for themselves; only we can come to their aid.... I asked these souls what their greatest suffering was. They answered me in one voice that their greatest torment was longing for God. I saw Our Lady visiting the souls in Purgatory. The souls call her "The Star of the Sea." She brings them refreshment.... [I heard an interior voice] which said, **My mercy does not want this, but justice demands it.** Since that time, I am in closer communion with the suffering souls. (*Diary*, 20)

Reflection

Most simply put, what's the torment of purgatory and what is it the souls there want? They long to see God. That's more than everything to them. It's the only thing. And like St. Faustina, we're called and chosen to be in "closer communion" with them. By our prayers and sacrifices we can help fulfill their most heartfelt—their most "soul-felt"—desire.

Prayer

Dear Lord, You who are Divine Mercy, have mercy on the souls in purgatory. Let them see You face-to-face, let them be with You forever.

Jesus, I trust in You.

November 6

TIME ... REVERSED

The days of suffering always seem longer, but they too will pass, though they pass so slowly that it seems they are moving backwards. However, their end is near, and then will come endless and inconceivable joy. Eternity! Who can understand this one word which comes from You, O incomprehensible God, this one word: eternity! (*Diary*, 578)

Reflection

Most people would agree that pain is slow and joy is fleeting. Or so it seems. And feels. What St. Faustina is reminding us is that pain *will* end. And, in the life to come, joy will be *forever*.

Prayer

Dear Holy Spirit, bring comfort to those who are nearing death, especially for N.

Jesus, I trust in You.

November 7

AN ELDERLY NUN IN COMBAT

Once, when visiting a sick sister who was eighty-four and known for many virtues, I asked her, "Sister, you are surely ready to stand before the Lord, are you not?" She answered, "I have been preparing myself all my life long for this last hour." And then she added, "Old age does not dispense one from the combat." (*Diary*, 517)

Reflection

The good news is someday we do "arrive." No more worries or troubles, no more temptations or suffering. It's part of the Good News Jesus came to share with us.

Prayer

Help me fight the good fight, Dear Lord. Help me finish the race. Help me keep the faith.

Jesus, I trust in You.

November 8

THROUGHOUT OUR LIFE

I realize more and more how much every soul needs God's mercy throughout life and particularly at the hour of death. This chaplet mitigates God's anger, as He Himself told me. (*Diary*, 1036)

Reflection

There's never a day, hour, or minute when we don't need God's mercy. There's never a moment when we, in some way, "earn" it. It's a gift freely given but one, through our prayers (such as the Chaplet of Divine Mercy), we can come to better accept and appreciate.

Prayer

Thank You, Most Generous God, for Your infinite mercy and love. Today I pray that N. will be more open to accepting both.

Jesus, I trust in You.

November 9

THEY CAN HEAR ME

I rejoiced greatly at the fact of how much the saints think of us and of how closely we are united with them. Oh, the goodness of God! How beautiful is the spiritual world, that already here on earth we commune with the saints! (*Diary*, 448)

Reflection

St. Faustina is telling us, "Yes, the saints can hear us." And not just canonized saints but our own loved ones, too. Those who have died are thinking of you. Are praying for you. Are loving you. And they're waiting ready to answer your prayers.

Prayer

What a gift, Dear Lord. What a blessing and a comfort. My loved ones who have died can hear me and pray for me. Can continue to love me. Thank You, Dear Lord, for the Communion of Saints.

Jesus, I trust in You.

November 10
NEGLECTING OUR RESPONSIBILITY

> Sister [Henry] was dying. A few days later she came to me [in spirit, after her death] and bid me to go to the Mother Directress of Novices [Sister Margaret] and tell her to ask her confessor, Father Rospond, to offer one Mass for her and three [Eternal Rest] prayers.... [O]n the third day this sister came to me and said, "May God repay you." (*Diary*, 21)

Reflection

It's not unusual that many wonderful things are said about the deceased at their funeral, and rightly so. But that can make us forget our duty, and privilege, to have Masses offered for them. And to keep them in our prayers. But then, too—we need to remember and thank them—they're keeping us in theirs, too.

Prayer

Eternal rest grant unto N., O Lord. And let perpetual light shine upon him/her. May his/her soul and all the souls of the faithful departed, through the mercy of God, rest in peace. Amen.

Jesus, I trust in You.

November 11

FOR THOSE WHO DON'T BELIEVE

O my God, how I pity those people who do not believe
in eternal life; how I pray for them that a ray of mercy
would envelop them too, and that God would clasp
them to His fatherly bosom. (*Diary*, 780)

Reflection

The death of a loved one and the inevitability of one's own death
can be so hard, so frightening, for those who don't know life on
earth isn't the end of life. The gift of faith, which tells us of eternal
life, comes with strings (or perhaps ribbons) attached. It demands
we keep in our prayers those who don't know Our Lord, don't know
their Lord, whose love for them is infinite. And, like their souls, is
eternal.

Prayer

Give Your peace to those who don't know You, Lord. Don't let their
hearts be troubled or afraid.

Jesus, I trust in You.

November 12
COMMITTING SUICIDE

Once, I took upon myself a terrible temptation which one of our students in the house at Warsaw was going through. It was the temptation of suicide. For seven days I suffered; and after the seven days Jesus granted her the grace which was being asked, and then my suffering also ceased. It was a great suffering. (*Diary*, 192)

Reflection

In the words of the *Catechism of the Catholic Church*: "Grave psychological disturbances, anguish, or grave fear of hardship, suffering, or torture can diminish the responsibility of the one committing suicide. We should not despair of the eternal salvation of persons who have taken their own lives. By ways known to him alone, God can provide the opportunity for salutary repentance. The Church prays for persons who have taken their own lives" (2282–2283). Yes, compared to St. Faustina's time, medical science and healthcare now know much about the causes and prevention of suicide. But now, as then, those who are suffering in this way need our prayers and support.

Prayer

Today, Dear Heavenly Father, I pray for those who are suicidal and for the souls of those who have taken their own lives. I pray, too, for all their loved ones.

Jesus, I trust in You.

November 13

SUPER(NATURAL) HEROES

When I immersed myself in prayer and united myself with all the Masses that were being celebrated all over the world at that time, I implored God, for the sake of all these Holy Masses, to have mercy on the world and especially on poor sinners who were dying at that moment. At the same instant, I received an interior answer from God that a thousand souls had received grace through the prayerful mediation I had offered to God. We do not know the number of souls that is ours to save through our prayers and sacrifices; therefore, let us always pray for sinners. (*Diary*, 1783)

Reflection

Today St. Faustina is telling us that we, like her, can be super(natural) heroes. Without lifting a finger, but by lifting our many prayers to heaven, we can help souls avoid hell. Amazing! Not that we *have* this power but that God allows us to share in the work of *His* power. How could we possibly pass up opportunities to do that?

Prayer

Thank You, Generous Father, for inviting me to play a role in the lives of those so close to the end of their time on earth. Have mercy on them, and on the whole world.

Jesus, I trust in You.

November 14

MERCY FOR THE JOURNEY

Oh, how much we should pray for the dying! Let us take advantage of mercy while there is still time for mercy. (*Diary*, 1035)

Reflection

It's not unusual that when we're saying something we consider important we repeat it. We say it at least twice so our listener is sure to hear it. St. Faustina wants us to hear what she says in today's quote and so, time and again throughout her *Diary*, she urges us to pray for the dying.

She urges us to pray for them *today*.

Prayer

Heavenly Father, be merciful to all those who are near death. This is for them: "Hail Mary, full of grace...."

Jesus, I trust in You.

November 15

NOT BY GREAT DEEDS

Now I understand why there are so few saints; it is because
so few souls are deeply humble. (*Diary*, 1306)

Reflection

There aren't many stories where the main character is noted for
his or her humility. We don't want meek heroes or heroines. We
admire protagonists with courage and skill and strength and ...
probably really good looks and a subtle sense of humor, too. A few
saints were known to be handsome or humorous, but that isn't what
made them saints. Some seemed to have no marketable skills. But
they all had the courage and strength to be "deeply humble." St.
Faustina says that's in short supply.

Prayer

Give me opportunities to be a little more humble today, Lord. And
help me avoid taking great pride in my humility!

Jesus, I trust in You.

November 16

"WHY AM I STILL HERE?"

I see that the will of God has not yet been fulfilled in me, and that is why I must live, for I know that if I fulfill everything the Lord has planned for me in this world, He will not leave me in exile any longer, for heaven is my home. But before we go to our Homeland, we must fulfill the will of God on earth; that is, trials and struggles must run their full course in us. (*Diary*, 897)

Reflection

It's a common question asked by those who have lived long lives and those whose health is frail or confining: "Why am I still here?" St. Faustina, after recovering from a recent bout of serious illness offers an answer that satisfied her. She had more to do because God had more for her to do. But, of course, we don't know what's on His "list," except that, most likely, there will be "trials and struggles." Again, it's accepting—and living—God's will for us. A will that, so many times, we just don't understand.

Prayer

Dear Blessed Mother, be with those who feel ready to die but haven't yet been called to heaven. Be with them now and at the hour of their deaths. Amen.

Jesus, I trust in You.

November 17

THE VALUE OF SUFFERING

Oh, if only the suffering soul knew how it is loved by God, it would die of joy and excess of happiness! Someday, we will know the value of suffering, but then we will no longer be able to suffer. The present moment is ours. (*Diary*, 963)

Reflection

"Mindfulness" is a popular concept these days. It's paying closer attention to oneself in the here and now. Not in a selfish way but in a way that notices all that's going on as we ... feel upset or enjoy a walk outside, for example. St. Faustina is saying, yes, the here and now may be a time of suffering but, only in the time to come beyond all time, will we see the huge and positive effect it had when we offered it up as a prayer for others.

Prayer

Holy Spirit, give me the strength to accept my pain and sorrows, and the wisdom to offer them up as prayers for others.

Jesus, I trust in You.

November 18

IN ALL THINGS, BE BLESSED

Bid me to stay in this convent, I will stay; bid me to undertake the work, I will undertake it; leave me in uncertainty about the work until I die, be blessed; give me death when, humanly speaking, my life seems particularly necessary, be blessed. Should You take me in my youth, be blessed; should You let me live to a ripe old age, be blessed. Should You give me health and strength, be blessed; should you confine me to a bed of pain for my whole life, be blessed. Should you give only failures and disappointments in life, be blessed. Should You allow my purest intentions to be condemned, be blessed. Should You enlighten my mind, be blessed. Should You leave me in darkness and all kinds of torments, be blessed. (*Diary*, 1264)

Reflection

What a beautiful—and brave—prayer. What a complete submission to the will of God. What a challenge for us to pray, and mean it.

Prayer

Bid me. Ask me. I want to say yes, to Your will for me, Lord. Always.

Jesus, I trust in You.

November 19

"LOVINGLY"!

[Jesus said to St. Faustina:] **Daughter, I need sacrifice lovingly accomplished, because that alone has meaning for Me. Enormous indeed are the debts of the world which are due to Me; pure souls can pay them by their sacrifice, exercising mercy in spirit.** (*Diary*, 1316)

Reflection

Why couldn't Jesus have just said, "I need sacrifice accomplished"? Why did He have to include "lovingly"? That pretty much eliminates doing it in a grumpy or sanctimonious way. And! We have to cover for others' "debts." It doesn't seem fair. But then again, thank God, God isn't fair. Imagine if He gave us what we deserved!

Prayer

Help me be a more-cheerful giver, Lord. And a more-appreciative receiver of the sacrifices You invite me to accept for the welfare of others.

Jesus, I trust in You.

November 20

JUST LIKE US

O souls, how I love you! (*Diary*, 1613)

Reflection

It's good to remember, to realize, that the souls in purgatory are *human*. That each is just like us except, until the end of time, their body is separated from their soul. Joe is still Joe. Mary is still Mary. Each is capable of loving and of receiving love. Each needs our prayers and we, in turn, can greatly benefit from theirs. Today, each is asking for your help. And each is anxious to help you.

Prayer

Eternal rest grant unto them, O Lord. Let them see You face-to-face.

Jesus, I trust in You.

November 21

SUFFERING FOR THE SUFFERING SOULS

Today the Lord said to me, **I have need of your sufferings to rescue souls.** (*Diary*, 1612)

Reflection

St. Faustina was no stranger to suffering, both from ill health and community life. What's amazing in today's quotation, written less than nine months before her death at the age of thirty-three, is Jesus telling her: "I have need." That was how important it was for her and for the holy souls in purgatory and on earth. Just as God allowed her to "transform" her suffering into a prayer for the souls on earth and in purgatory. He does the same for us. What can I offer up today for them?

Prayer

Thank You, Lord, for letting my suffering—my pain, my heartache, my tears and disappointments—be prayers for my loved ones in purgatory preparing to enter heaven. For the souls on earth most in need of prayer. Divine Mercy, bring us home.

Jesus, I trust in You.

November 22

"SECRET" PRAYERS

During adoration, I heard these words: **Pray for one of the students who has great need of My grace.** And I recognized N. I prayed hard, and God's mercy embraced that soul. (*Diary*, 1603)

Reflection

It can be comforting and more than a little disconcerting—a bit scary—to realize God invites each of us to pray for a particular person on earth or soul in purgatory. But He does. Our task is to listen, to have faith in the One who has so much faith in us, and to offer that prayer. Who is that person, that soul, today?

Prayer

Heavenly Father, today I pray for N.

Jesus, I trust in You.

November 23

HOW TO SHOW HIM?

God made known to me what true love consists in and gave
light to me about how, in practice, to give proof of it to
Him. True love of God consists in carrying out God's will.
To show God our love in what we do, all our actions, even
the least, must spring from our love of God. (*Diary*, 279)

Reflection

In today's quote St. Faustina asks how we can show our love
for God? Her answer—a theme she comes back to again and
again—is: 1. Carry out God's will. 2. Let all our actions, even the
smallest, "spring from our love of God." That's proof positive!

Prayer

Dear Jesus, You ask me, as You asked St. Peter, "Do you love Me?"
Help my actions show my love for You. Help me feed Your lambs,
and feed Your sheep.

Jesus, I trust in You.

November 24

GREAT PATIENCE

With great patience, I will listen when others open their hearts to me, accept their sufferings, give them spiritual comfort, but drown my own sufferings in the most merciful Heart of Jesus. (*Diary*, 1550)

Reflection

It can be so hard to listen to someone go on and on about their own troubles when, it seems to us, those problems aren't nearly as bad as the ones we face. The ones we live with. Today St. Faustina doesn't say doing that kind of listening doesn't require *just* "patience" but can demand "*great* patience." And, of course, she's right. Where could she turn? Where can we? To the "most merciful Heart of Jesus."

Prayer

Give me great patience, Dear Jesus, when others open their hearts to me and speak of their sufferings. And thank You for always so, so patiently listening to me!

Jesus, I trust in You.

November 25
WANTING TO DO GOOD

... I received an inner understanding of the great reward
that God is preparing for us, not only for our good
deeds, but also for our sincere desire to perform them.
What a great grace of God this is! (*Diary*, 450)

Reflection

St. Faustina says, the road to heaven isn't paved just with perform-
ing good deeds, but also with our sincere desire to perform them. A
double blessing. (A smoother ride.) One for the doing, one for the
wanting to do.

Prayer

Dear Lord, help me be not just a cheerful giver but a cheerful doer.
Jesus, I trust in You.

November 26

LOVE LIVES ON

All things will have an end in this vale of tears,
Tears will run dry and pain will cease.
Only one thing will remain—
Love for You, O Lord. (*Diary*, 1132)

Reflection

In today's quote St. Faustina offers the encouraging, and true, point that there will come a day, a time, when your pain and your tears will end. Your worries and grief will ... stop. What will continue and expand? The love you have for God, and your awareness of the love He has for you!

Prayer

Dear Lord, I pray for those who are grieving, for those whose days and nights are filled with tears.

Jesus, I trust in You.

November 27

THE KING OF HEARTS

Today is the Feast of Christ the King.... I prayed fervently
that Jesus might become King of all hearts and that
divine grace might shine in every soul. (*Diary*, 500)

Reflection

Jesus—Christ the King—told us we can be His brothers and
sisters, if.... "Whoever does the will of my Father in heaven is my
brother, and sister ..." (Mt 12:50).

Prayer

Lord, You're inviting me to be a part of Your Royal Family. How
could I say no to that?

Jesus, I trust in You.

November 28

A GLIMMER OF GRACE

All grace flows from mercy, and the last hour abounds with mercy for us. Let no one doubt concerning the goodness of God; even if a person's sins were as dark as night, God's mercy is stronger than our misery. One thing alone is necessary: that the sinner set ajar the door of his heart, be it ever so little, to let in a ray of God's merciful grace, and then God will do the rest. (*Diary*, 1507)

Reflection

We're used to asking Mary to pray for us at the hour of our death, but St. Faustina offers an additional image. At the hour of their death, if someone even just barely cracks the door of their heart, God's love and mercy will come flooding in. We never have to—or are able to—"meet God halfway." We can only take small, faltering steps toward Him, and "then God will do the rest."

Prayer

Heavenly Father, let all those facing the hour of their death today "set ajar the door" of their hearts. Let them, by Your love and mercy, enter and live in Your kingdom forever.

Jesus, I trust in You.

November 29

THE 9K NOVENA

> I prepared [for the Solemnity of the Immaculate Conception]
> not only by means of the novena said in common by the
> whole community, but I also made a personal effort to
> salute Her a thousand times each day, saying a thousand
> "Hail Marys" for nine days in Her praise. (*Diary*, 1413)

Reflection

Notice neither Jesus nor Mary nor St. Faustina is telling us to pray
one thousand Hail Marys a day for nine days. That was for St. Faustina's personal goal. For us, for our "personal novena," perhaps it's
ten a day. Perhaps it's singing one Marian hymn daily. Perhaps it's
meditating, "pondering," on Mary's life for a few minutes and then
considering how, on that day, we can imitate her. No doubt, Jesus,
Mary, and St. Faustina are confident we can come up with something that's just right.

Prayer

Immaculate Mary, your praises I sing! *Ave Maria*, my dear Mother.
Jesus, I trust in You.

November 30

A SNEAK PEEK

During meditation, the Lord gave me knowledge of the joy of heaven and of the saints on our arrival there; they love God as the sole object of their love, but they also have a tender and heartfelt love for us. It is from the face of God that this joy flows, out upon all, because we see Him face to face. His face is so sweet that the soul falls anew into ecstasy. (*Diary*, 1592)

Reflection

It would be interesting, and embarrassing, to know how often we daydream of winning the lottery compared to daydreaming of entering heaven. Maybe part of it is because we can imagine what we'd do with all that money, but what with all that ... grace? St. Faustina gives us a peek: here's what it's like when someone enters heaven. Deep joy for those who have a "tender and heartfelt love for us." Our family, our friends, and others. The perfect reunion, that never ends. In the meantime ... how am I treating family, friends, and others still with me here on earth?

Prayer

I pray for those who have died and are now being readied to enter heaven. Those growing in love in purgatory. Please let them join that heavenly banquet soon.

Jesus, I trust in You.

CHAPTER TWELVE

Reflections

FOR

December

December 1

AN *ADVENT* RESOLUTION

Advent is approaching. I want to prepare my heart for the coming of the Lord Jesus by silence and recollection of spirit, uniting myself with the Most Holy Mother and faithfully imitating Her virtue of silence, by which She found pleasure in the eyes of God Himself. I trust that, by Her side, I will persevere in this resolution. (*Diary*, 1398)

Reflection

Most of us like to put off making resolutions involving self-improvement for as long as possible. And then we quickly forget them. In today's quote it seems St. Faustina is jumping the gun a little and not waiting for New Year's. She has a wonderful idea here: *Advent* resolutions. What better way to prepare for Christmas? And with a wreath and four candles as reminders!

Prayer

O come, O come, Emmanuel. I want to come closer to the person You created me to be.

Jesus, I trust in You.

December 2
FRIENDS IN THE FAITH

My Jesus, how little these people talk about You. They talk about everything but You, Jesus. And if they talk so little [about You], it is quite probable that they do not think about You at all. The whole world interests them; but about You, their Creator, there is silence. Jesus, I am sad to see this great indifference and ingratitude of creatures. O my Jesus, I want to love You for them and to make atonement to You, by my love. (*Diary*, 804)

Reflection

What a delight, what a blessing, to find others willing to talk about their love of God and listen to us speaking of ours. As when the two or three are gathered in His name to pray, He is in their midst, so too when they gather to share with each other and grow in the faith.

Prayer

Thank You, Lord, for the people in my life who know You and love You. Being with them is a true blessing.

Jesus, I trust in You.

December 3

THE SECRET TO HAPPINESS ON EARTH

If there is a truly happy soul upon earth, it can
only be a truly humble soul. (*Diary*, 593)

Reflection

It's good to notice that sometimes the Lord can be pretty clever.
Hiding happiness in humility, and joy in service to others. It's good
to remember He wants our lives to be filled with both, and so He
tells us where, and how, to look for each.

Prayer

Thank you, Dear Jesus, for sharing the "clues" to happiness and joy
on earth.

Jesus, I trust in You.

December 4
THE GREATEST GREATNESS

I know well, O Lord, that You have no need of our works;
You demand love. Love, love, and once again, love of God.
There is nothing greater in heaven or on earth. The greatest
greatness is to love God; true greatness is in loving God; real
wisdom is to love God. All that is great and beautiful is in God;
there is no beauty or greatness outside of Him. O you sages of
the world and you great minds, recognize that true greatness
is in loving God! Oh, how astonished I am that some people
deceive themselves, saying: There is no eternity! (*Diary*, 990)

Reflection

It shouldn't be surprising that nothing can surpass what's infinite, all-powerful, and eternal. *Who's* infinite, all-powerful, and eternal. Still
… swept up in this world we can lose sight of that. Can, at times,
forget it. And what does God ask of us? Love. Just love. Only love.

Prayer

Father, Son, and Holy Spirit, I love You. Help me better love You
by better loving—and helping—others.

Jesus, I trust in You.

December 5

CARRYING OUR LOAD

O Christ, although much effort is required, all things can be done with Your grace. (*Diary*, 1696)

Reflection

Today's quote seems a little like the "fine print" added to the familiar Scripture passage that "with God all things are possible" (Mt 19:26). Yes, but "much effort is required." Presumably not by God, but by ... us. St. Faustina, for all her visions and insights and mysticism, was a pretty hardcore realist. God does the heavy lifting, but our hands aren't supposed to be empty and our backs aren't supposed to be burden-free.

Prayer

Help me share the load, Lord. And forgive me for the times I grumble about having to do it.

Jesus, I trust in You.

December 6

FEAST OF ST. NICHOLAS

THE "NOW" OF CHILDREN

... [M]y confessor told me to reflect upon this spiritual childhood. It was somewhat difficult at first, but my confessor, disregarding my difficulties, told me to continue to reflect upon spiritual childhood. "In practice, this spiritual childhood," [he said,] "should manifest itself in this way: a child does not worry about the past or the future, but makes use of the present moment. I want to emphasize that spiritual childlikeness in you, Sister, and I place great stress upon it." (*Diary*, 333)

Reflection

It wasn't just St. Faustina's confessor who spoke of "childlike" spirituality but Jesus himself. "Truly, I say to you, unless you turn and become like children, you will never enter the kingdom of heaven. Whoever humbles himself like this child, he is the greatest in the kingdom of heaven" (Mt 18:3–4). The two keys for us? Focusing on today, not the past or the future. And taking humility seriously.

Prayer

Thank You for making spirituality simple, Lord. Simple but, I know, not easy.

Jesus, I trust in You.

December 7
TWO GIFTS IN ONE

Concerning Holy Confession. We should derive two kinds of profit from Holy Confession: 1. We come to confession to be healed; 2. We come to be educated—like a small child, our soul has constant need of education. (*Diary*, 377)

Reflection

We may never have looked at the confessional as a classroom but that's what St. Faustina is telling us it is. Yes, there's a spiritual healing but there are also lessons to be learned. (Or relearned.) The more educated in Christ we become, the more we can see sinning as so very foolish. Always. And, through confession, we can equip ourselves with more spiritual tools to help us turn away from it.

Prayer

Thank You, Merciful Jesus, for giving me so many gifts, and for so many times You've welcomed me back with open arms.

Jesus, I trust in You.

December 8

SO LOVELY AND SO BEAUTIFUL

From early morning, I felt the nearness of the Blessed Mother. During Holy Mass, I saw Her, so lovely and so beautiful that I have no words to express even a small part of this beauty. She was all [in] white, with a blue sash around Her waist. Her cloak was also blue, and there was a crown on Her head. Marvelous light streamed forth from Her whole figure. *I am the Queen of heaven and earth,* . . . Now I understand why I have been preparing for this feast for two months and have been looking forward to it with such yearning. From today onwards, I am going to strive for the greatest purity of soul, that the rays of God's grace may be reflected in all their brilliance. I long to be a crystal in order to find favor in His eyes. (*Diary*, 805)

Reflection

The beauty of the Blessed Virgin, chosen to be the Mother of God, isn't just skin deep. It's *soul* deep.

Prayer

Beautiful Mother of God, and my Mother, thank you.
   Jesus, I trust in You.

December 9

FEAST OF ST. JUAN DIEGO

LOOKING FOR LOOPHOLES

It is impossible for one to please God without
obeying His holy will. (*Diary*, 1244)

Reflection

We love loopholes. There *has* to be a way around something we
don't want to do, right? And God lets us choose, of course, knowing if we ignore His will we're saying no to a better life. Plus, St.
Faustina teaches, we're passing up an opportunity to please Him.

Prayer

Oh, Lord, be patient with me when I try to wiggle out of things
You're asking me to do. Help me remember You *really* know what
You're doing: always what's best for me.

Jesus, I trust in You.

December 10

WHY SHOULD I . . . ?

> . . . Jesus alone is the motive for my love of neighbor. (*Diary*, 871)

Reflection

It isn't just little kids (and teens!) who can constantly ask Mom and Dad, "Why?" Why do I have to . . . ? Why can't I . . . ? At times, no matter our age, we're that way to our Heavenly Father. What does He ask of us? Love. Serve. Forgive. Why? Jesus.

Prayer

Father, You didn't just send a Son and Redeemer, You sent an example. Help me follow in His footsteps.

Jesus, I trust in You.

December 11

EXPECT LITTLE, GIVE MUCH

My Master, cause my heart never to expect help from anyone,
but I will always strive to bring assistance, consolation
and all manner of relief to others. (*Diary*, 871)

Reflection

Yes, "Every one to whom much is given, of him will much be
required" (Lk 12:48), but, St. Faustina points out, we may get very
little support from others to meet our "requirement." Many may
talk the talk, but saints — and those on the path to holiness — walk
the walk. That is, "bring assistance, consolation and all manner of
relief to others."

Prayer

Lord, help me be an example of the joy that accompanies giving.
   Jesus, I trust in You.

December 12
JOY FOR OTHERS

The happiness of other souls fills me with a new joy, and when I see the higher gifts in some soul, my heart soars up to the Lord in a new hymn of adoration. (*Diary*, 1671)

Reflection

One of the (infinite) benefits of having an all-loving God is that there's no limit to that love, no losing some of His love for *me* because He began to love *someone else* more. As St. Faustina says, the happiness of someone else doesn't cut a slice out of her own happiness. Just the opposite. It makes her happier. Their joy gives her more joy, new joy. Simply put, there's enough God to go around for everyone. So why, at times, are we selfish with our love?

Prayer

Dear Lord, help me love more like You do. Help me love more generously.

Jesus, I trust in You.

December 13

BREAKING BREAD

> I am never alone, because He [God] is my constant companion.
> He is present to me at every moment. (*Diary*, 318)

Reflection

You may know that "companion" come from two Latin words meaning "to break bread with." St. Faustina had been writing about receiving Holy Communion and then went on to point out that because of the Eucharist she felt Our Lord's presence throughout the day. But, of course, Jesus is more than someone with whom we break bread. He *is* the bread, too. The Bread of Life. With you, right here, right now.

Prayer

Thank You, Sweet Jesus, that You aren't just a memory or historical figure. Thank You that You're truly present when we "do this in memory of" You.

Jesus, I trust in You.

December 14

NO HIDDEN MOTIVES

> ... [T]he Lord gave me an understanding of God's incomprehensible love for people. He lifts us up to His very Godhead. His only motives are love and fathomless mercy. (*Diary*, 1172)

Reflection

The private investigator frequently talks about means, motive, and opportunity to find who they're looking for. What can we discover about God by focusing on those three areas? Yes, as a Supreme Being, He has the means to do ... anything. And, St. Faustina tells us, "His only motives are love and fathomless mercy." But what about opportunity? That's where we come in. God gives us countless opportunities to help Him do His work on earth.

Prayer

Heavenly Father, I want to help others find their way to You.

Jesus, I trust in You.

December 15

ST. FAUSTINA'S BEDTIME PRAYER

Good night, my Jesus; the bell is calling me to sleep....
Good night, my Beloved; I rejoice at being one day closer
to eternity. And if You let me wake up tomorrow, Jesus, I
shall begin a new hymn to Your praise. (*Diary*, 679)

Reflection

What a beautiful, tender, personal prayer! What a wonderful way
to say "good night." And ... what a wonderful way to make plans
for the next day: from the moment of awakening, to "begin a new
hymn to Your praise."

Prayer

Praise be to You, Heavenly Father. Praise be to You, Beloved Son.
Praise be to You, Holy Spirit. All praise be to You, Triune God. All
praise, always.

Jesus, I trust in You.

December 16
IN TWO WORDS

God is love, and His Spirit is peace. (*Diary*, 589)

Reflection

God's love and peace. What more could we ask for? What more could we need?

Prayer

Dear God, help me show love to those who feel unloved. Holy Spirit, bring peace to those with troubled minds, hearts, or souls.

Jesus, I trust in You.

December 17

"BITE YOUR TONGUE"

I tremble to think that I have to give an account of my tongue. There is life, but there is also death in the tongue. Sometimes we kill with the tongue: we commit real murders. And we are still to regard that as a small thing? I truly do not understand such consciences. I have known a person who, when she learned from someone that a certain thing was being said about her, fell seriously ill.... It was not the sword that did all this, but the tongue. (*Diary*, 119)

Reflection

During his December 2017 visit to Bangladesh, Pope Francis said, "There is one image I like to use in describing the spirit of gossip. It is terrorism ... because those who speak ill of others do not do so publicly. The terrorist does not say publicly: 'I'm a terrorist.'

"And those who speak ill of others, do so in secret.

"Dear sister, dear brother, when you want to speak ill of another person, bite your tongue! Most probably, it will swell up, but you will not wrong your brother or your sister."

Prayer

Mum's the word, Lord.

Jesus, I trust in You.

December 18

GOD'S MAJESTY

When I entered the chapel, once again the majesty of God overwhelmed me. I felt that I was immersed in God, totally immersed in Him and penetrated by Him, being aware of how much the heavenly Father loves us. (*Diary*, 491)

Reflection

Perhaps we don't take the time, or make the time, to "totally immerse" ourselves in Him. What if we did, perhaps not totally, but at least a little bit more?

Prayer

Today, Lord, help me do what the psalmist advises: "Let us come into his presence with thanksgiving; let us make a joyful noise to him with songs of praise!" (Ps 95:2).

Jesus, I trust in You.

December 19

HEAVEN ISN'T BORING

Today I was in heaven, in spirit, and I saw its inconceivable beauties and the happiness that awaits us after death.... This source of happiness is unchanging in its essence, but it is always new, gushing forth happiness for all creatures. Now I understand Saint Paul, who said, "Eye has not seen, nor has ear heard, nor has it entered into the heart of man what God has prepared for those who love Him." (*Diary*, 777)

Reflection

It's a common question: What do you think heaven's like? Yes, it's face-to-face with God. But as mortal human beings here on earth, we sometimes wonder: that's it? St. Faustina and St. Paul assure us "It's always new," the nun says. "You can't even imagine it," says the apostle. Both agree. It's inconceivable.

Prayer

Heaven is just one more mystery that demands my patience, for now. I trust You with the details, Dear Lord.

Jesus, I trust in You.

December 20

FOR AS LONG AS WE LIVE

> As long as we live, the love of God grows in us. Until we die, we ought to strive for the love of God. (*Diary*, 1191)

Reflection

With every breath we take, with every act of kindness we perform, with every prayer we say, with every sacrifice for others we make, God's love grows in us. There is no "full, all done," only "more, more, more." From here to eternity.

Prayer

Dear Heavenly Father, thank You for being the "God of More."

Jesus, I trust in You.

December 21

GOD OF ALL GOODNESS

God's Infinite Goodness in Creating Mankind. God, who in Your mercy have deigned to call man from nothingness into being, generously have You bestowed upon him nature and grace. But that seemed too little for Your infinite goodness. In Your mercy, O Lord, You have given us everlasting life. You admit us to Your everlasting happiness and grant us to share in Your interior life. And You do this solely out of Your mercy. You bestow on us the gift of Your grace, only because You are good and full of love. You had no need of us at all to be happy, but You, O Lord, want to share Your own happiness with us. (*Diary*, 1743)

Reflection

In her prayer of praise, St. Faustina does a wonderful job on describing what God has done — and what He continues to do. Yes, for all mankind, but for *each* of us. For you. Nature, grace, mercy, and everlasting life. Everlasting happiness and a sharing in His interior life.

Prayer

God of All Goodness, I praise You. God of All Goodness, I thank You. God of All Goodness, I love You.

Jesus, I trust in You.

December 22

A LIFETIME OF DOING GOOD

> O Jesus, I understand Your mercy is beyond all imagining, and
> therefore, I ask You to make my heart so big that there will be room
> in it for the needs of all souls living on the face of the earth ...
> help me to go through life doing good to everyone. (*Diary*, 692)

Reflection

St. Faustina wants to "go through life doing good." How does she
do it?

Begin with a merciful heart, like Jesus.

Prayer

Dear Lord, help me quietly—and humbly—do the good You're
calling me to do.

Jesus, I trust in You.

December 23

HE DELIGHTS IN ME

> I do not know how to live without God, but I also
> feel that God, absolutely self-sufficient though He is,
> cannot be happy without me ... (*Diary*, 1120)

Reflection

There come times and point where mystics and visionaries part ways with theologians and Scripture scholars. This is one of them. God's "absolutely self-sufficient" but somehow — through His grace and generosity — He "cannot be happy without me." Each of us, too, can "add to His joy." The psalmist put it this way: "He brought me forth into a broad place; he delivered me, because he delighted in me" (18:19).

Prayer

Dear God, help me be more delightful in Your eyes.

Jesus, I trust in You.

December 24

ON THE NIGHT BEFORE CHRISTMAS

December 24, 1934. The Vigil of Christmas.... [That evening, in the chapel,] [f]rom nine to ten o'clock I offered my adoration for my parents and my whole family. From ten to eleven, I offered it for the intention of my spiritual director ... And from eleven to twelve I prayed for the Holy Church and the clergy, for sinners, for the missions, and for our houses. I offered the indulgences for the souls in purgatory. (*Diary*, 346)

Reflection

What a wonderful idea. On the night before Christmas — and, oh, what a whirlwind that can be — to take a few moments to pray for our loved ones, for those who help us in so many ways, and for the souls in purgatory who can't pray for themselves. What a gift for each group. No wrapping necessary.

Prayer

Holy Family, bless my family and loved ones. St. John Vianney, patron of parish priests, intercede for all those who minister to others. Blessed Mother, Star of the Sea, lead the holy souls from purgatory to life eternal in heaven.

Jesus, I trust in You.

December 25

WITH ARMS STRETCHED

I said to [the Infant Jesus in my arms], "I know that You are my Lord and Creator even though You are so tiny." Jesus stretched His little arms out to me and looked at me with a smile. My spirit was filled with incomparable joy. (*Diary*, 609)

Reflection

St. Faustina wrote of a couple of times that Mary handed the Infant Jesus to her. In this instance, she's delighted and overwhelmed when He smiles and lifts His "little arms" to her. Now ascended, Our Lord extends His arms to us in love and mercy, and smiles on us.

Prayer

Thank You for always welcoming me with open arms, Dear Jesus. Thank You for smiling on me.

Jesus, I trust in You.

December 26

O GOD, WE PRAISE YOU

... I asked the Lord, "Why are You treating him like that?" [Father Sopocko]. The Lord answered me that it was for the triple crown meant for him: that of virginity, the priesthood and martyrdom. At that moment, a great joy flooded my soul at the sight of the great glory that is going to be his in heaven. Right away I said the *Te Deum* for this special grace of God; namely, of learning how God treats those He intends to have close to himself. Thus, all sufferings are nothing in comparison with what awaits us in heaven. (*Diary*, 596)

Reflection

As you may know, the *Te Deum* is an early Christian hymn of praise sung on joyful occasions. The title's taken from its opening words in Latin: *Te Deum laudamus*, "O God, we praise You."

How can I, through my words and by my actions, praise God today?

Prayer

(From the *Te Deum*)

O God, we praise You, and acknowledge You to be the supreme Lord.

Everlasting Father, all the earth worships You.

All the Angels ... continuously cry to You:

Holy, Holy, Holy, Lord God of Hosts!

Heaven and earth are full of the Majesty of Your glory.

The glorious choir of the Apostles,

The wonderful company of Prophets,

The white-robed army of Martyrs, praise You.

Holy Church throughout the world acknowledges You:

The Father of infinite Majesty;

Your adorable, true and only Son;

Also the Holy Spirit, the Comforter.

O Christ, You are the King of glory! ...

Jesus, I trust in You.

December 27

FEAST OF ST. JOHN THE EVANGELIST

JOINING CHOIRS OF ANGELS

O King of Glory, though You hide Your beauty, yet the eye of my soul rends the veil. I see the angelic choirs giving You honor without cease, and all the heavenly Powers praising You without cease, and without cease they are saying: Holy, Holy, Holy. (*Diary*, 80)

Reflection

So, at the end of the Offertory at Mass, there you are, pray-ing—singing!—with angelic choirs. Heaven and earth are filled with God's glory ... and with the praises of the angels and you. And God sees that it is good.

Prayer

Holy, holy, holy, Lord God of hosts, I praise you!

Jesus, I trust in You.

December 28

FEAST OF THE HOLY INNOCENTS

THE TEARS OF CHILDREN

I beg You, Jesus, look not on our sins, but on the tears of little children, on the hunger and cold they suffer. Jesus, for the sake of these innocent ones, grant me the grace that I am asking of You for my country." At that moment, I saw the Lord Jesus, His eyes filled with tears, and He said to me, **You see, My daughter, what great compassion I have for them. Know that it is they who uphold the world.** (*Diary*, 286)

Reflection

The power of St. Faustina's words capture the image of Our Lord. "His eyes filled with tears."

Yes, we are to pray for our country, but our concern is to be for more than that.

It's to be for every child everywhere. To regularly remember them in our prayers.

Prayer

Heavenly Father, help Your youngest sons and daughters. Help me help them, too.

Jesus, I trust in You.

December 29

HOLD THE BABY

During Mass, God's presence pierced me through and through. A moment before the Elevation I saw the Mother of God and the Infant Jesus and the good Old Man [St. Joseph]. The Most Holy Mother spoke these words to me: *My daughter, Faustina, take this most precious Treasure*, and she gave me the Infant Jesus. When I took Jesus in my arms, my soul felt such unspeakable joy that I am unable to describe it. (*Diary*, 846)

Reflection

What a generous and trusting new Mother. "Here, St. Faustina, would you like to hold the baby?" Would she! It's easy to imagine the look on her face even made "the good Old Man" smile. In St. Faustina's vision, and now in our own lives, Jesus, Mary, and Joseph invite us to join their family.

Prayer

Jesus, Mary, and Joseph, I give you my heart and my soul. Jesus, Mary, and Joseph, may I die in your blessed company.

Jesus, I trust in You.

December 30

THE GOODNESS OF JESUS

> Whatever Jesus did, He did well. He went along, doing
> good. His manner was full of goodness and mercy. His
> steps were guided by compassion. Toward His enemies
> He showed goodness, kindness, and understanding, and
> to those in need help and consolation. (*Diary*, 1175)

Reflection

Amid all the lofty and deeply theological ways St. Faustina describes Jesus, it's a little startling to read today's quote. Yes, He was and is God, but also a wonderful human being. One any of us would want to have as a friend. The kind of person, the kind of friend, we were created to be. And which—ah, here's the catch—we *can* be, too. Being a good man or a good woman is ... Christlike.

Prayer

I want us to become better friends, Jesus.

Jesus, I trust in You.

December 31

AND NOW SHE DOES

> ... I would like to cry out to the whole world, "Love God, because He is good and great is His mercy!" (*Diary*, 1372)

Reflection

Good news, Sister Faustina! You succeeded, probably beyond your wildest dreams. Your words—Christ's word to you—are being cried out to the whole world. (Including in books like this!) Now we listen as you tell us why to love God. Now we believe you and are strengthened by you when you remind us that "He is good and great is His mercy!"

Prayer

Give me "St. Faustina faith," Lord, when You ask me to do something that seems beyond my courage.

Jesus, I trust in You.

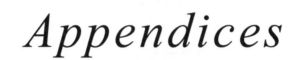

Appendices

The Divine Mercy Promises

Throughout her *Diary*, St. Faustina recorded promises Jesus made *not only to her but to those who would pray to, promote, and trust in Divine Mercy.*

To those souls who venerate the image of Divine Mercy

"I promise that the soul that will venerate this image will not perish. I also promise victory over [its] enemies already here on earth, especially at the hour of death. I Myself will defend it as My own glory." (*Diary*, 48)

To those souls who pray the Chaplet of Divine Mercy

"The souls that say this chaplet will be embraced by My mercy during their lifetime and especially at the hour of their death." (*Diary*, 754)

"When hardened sinners say it, I will fill their souls with peace, and the hour of their death will be a happy one." (*Diary*, 1541)

"... [W]hen they say this chaplet in the presence of the dying, I will stand between My Father and the dying person, not as the just Judge but as the merciful Savior." (*Diary*, 1541)

"Whoever will recite it will receive great mercy at the hour of death.... Even if there were a sinner most hardened, if he were to recite this chaplet only once, he would receive grace from My infinite mercy." (*Diary*, 687)

To those souls who honor and spread the worship of Divine Mercy

"I Myself will defend as My own glory, during their lifetime, and especially at the hour of their death, those souls who will venerate My fathomless mercy." (*Diary*, 1225)

"... All those souls who will glorify My mercy and spread its worship, encouraging others to trust in My mercy, will not experience terror at the hour of death. My mercy will shield them in that final battle." (*Diary*, 1540)

"Souls who spread the honor of My mercy I shield through their entire lives as a tender mother her infant, and at the hour of death I will not be a Judge for them, but the merciful Savior.... Happy is the soul that during its lifetime immersed itself in the Fountain of Mercy, because justice will have no hold on it." (*Diary*, 1075)

To those souls who put their trust in Divine Mercy

"He who trusts in My mercy will not perish, for all his affairs are Mine, and his enemies will be shattered at the base of My footstool." (*Diary*, 723)

"Souls that make an appeal to My mercy delight Me. To such souls I grant even more graces than they ask." (*Diary*, 1146)

"Every soul believing and trusting in My mercy will obtain it." (*Diary*, 420)

To those souls who honor the Hour of Mercy

"This is the hour of great mercy for the whole world. I will allow you to enter into My mortal sorrow. In this hour, I will refuse nothing to the soul that makes a request of Me in virtue of My Passion ..." (*Diary*, 1320)

To priests who proclaim and extol the Divine Mercy

"To priests who proclaim and extol My mercy, I will give wondrous power; I will anoint their words and touch the hearts of those to whom they will speak." (*Diary*, 1521)

Our Lord's Promises Attached to the Praying of the Chaplet of Divine Mercy as Revealed to St. Faustina

In addition to verses shared with the Divine Mercy Promises (*Diary*, 48, 754, 1541, 687, 1521, and 1387), the Promises Attached to the Praying of the Chaplet also include:

"At three o'clock, implore My mercy, especially for sinners; and, if only for a brief moment, immerse yourself in My Passion, particularly in My abandonment at the moment of agony. This is the hour of great mercy for the whole world. I will allow you to enter into My mortal sorrow. In this hour, I will refuse nothing to the soul that makes a request of me in virtue of My Passion ..." (*Diary*, 1320; also cf. 1572)

"Souls who spread the honor of My mercy ... at the hour of death I will not be a Judge for them, but the Merciful Savior." (*Diary*, 1075)

"The two rays denote Blood and Water.... These two rays issued from the very depths of My tender mercy when My agonized Heart was opened by a lance on the Cross. These rays shield souls from the wrath of My Father ... I desire that the first Sunday after Easter be the Feast of Mercy.... [W]hoever approaches the Fount of Life on this day will be granted complete remission of sins and punishment.

Mankind will not have peace until it turns with trust to My mercy." (*Diary*, 299–300)

"I desire that the Feast of Mercy be a refuge and shelter for all souls.... The soul that will go to Confession and receive Holy Communion (in a state of grace on this day) shall obtain complete forgiveness of sins and punishment.... It is My desire that [the Feast] be solemnly celebrated on the first Sunday after Easter...." (*Diary*, 699)

"Through this chaplet you will obtain everything, if what you ask for is compatible with My will." (*Diary*, 1731)

"My mercy is greater than your sins and those of the entire world." (*Diary*, 1485)

The Chaplet of Divine Mercy

[Jesus said to St. Faustina:] **Say unceasingly the chaplet that I have taught you. Whoever will recite it will receive great mercy at the hour of death.** *(Diary, 687)*

Traditionally, a five-decade rosary is used for praying the Divine Mercy Chaplet.

1. Begin with the Sign of the Cross, one Our Father, one Hail Mary, and the Apostles' Creed.

2. On the Our Father bead pray:

   Eternal Father, I offer You the Body and Blood, Soul and Divinity of Your dearly beloved Son, Our Lord Jesus Christ, in atonement for our sins and those of the whole world.

3. On the ten Hail Mary beads pray:

   For the sake of His sorrowful Passion, have mercy on us and on the whole world.

(Repeat steps 2 and 3 for all five decades).

4. After the fifth decade, conclude the chaplet by praying
   three times:

*Holy God, Holy Mighty One, Holy Immortal One, have
mercy on us and on the whole world.*

A Prayer Jesus Taught to St. Faustina

"[Jesus said to St. Faustina:] I desire that you know more profoundly
the love that burns in My Heart for souls, and you will understand
this when you meditate upon My Passion. Call upon My mercy on
behalf of sinners; I desire their salvation. When you say this prayer,
with a contrite heart and with faith on behalf of some sinner, I will
give him the grace of conversion. This is the prayer:

"O Blood and Water, which gushed forth from the Heart of
Jesus as a fount of Mercy for us, I trust in You." (*Diary*, 186–187)

A Novena to the Divine Mercy for the Conversion of the World

On Good Friday, 1937, Jesus requested that St. Faustina make a special novena. "... I am to begin it for the conversion of the whole world and for the recognition of The Divine Mercy ... [Jesus tells St. Faustina] ... so that every soul will praise My goodness. I desire trust from My creatures. Encourage souls to place great trust in My fathomless mercy. Let the weak, sinful soul have no fear to approach Me, for even if it had more sins than there are grains of sand in the world, all would be drowned in the unmeasurable depths of My mercy. (*Diary*, 1059)

The Lord dictated the intentions for each day. Faustina was to bring to His heart a different group of souls each day and immerse them in the ocean of His mercy.

Jesus to St. Faustina: I desire that during these nine days you bring souls to the fountain of My mercy, that they may draw therefrom strength and refreshment and whatever grace they need in the hardships of life, and especially at the hour of death. (*Diary*, 1209)

First Day

Today, bring to Me all mankind, especially all sinners.... (see *Diary*, 1210)

Most Merciful Jesus, whose very nature it is to have compassion on us and to forgive us, do not look upon our sins but upon our trust which we place in Your infinite goodness. Receive us all into the abode of Your Most Compassionate Heart, and never let us escape from it. We beg this of You by Your love which unites You to the Father and the Holy Spirit....

Eternal Father, turn Your merciful gaze upon all mankind and especially upon poor sinners, all enfolded in the Most Compassionate Heart of Jesus. For the sake of His sorrowful Passion, show us Your mercy, that we may praise the omnipotence of Your mercy forever and ever. Amen. (*Diary*, 1211)

Second Day

Today bring to Me the souls of priests and religious.... (*Diary*, 1212)

Most merciful Jesus, from whom comes all that is good, increase Your grace in us, that we may perform worthy works of mercy, and that all who see them may glorify the Father of Mercy who is in heaven....

Eternal Father, turn your merciful gaze upon the company [of chosen ones] in Your vineyard—upon the souls of priests and religious; and endow them with the strength of Your blessing. For the love of the Heart of Your Son in which they are enfolded, impart to them Your power and light, that they may be able to guide others in the way of salvation, and with one voice sing praise to Your boundless mercy for ages without end. Amen. (*Diary*, 1213)

Third Day

Today bring to Me all devout and faithful souls.... (*Diary*, 1214)

Most Merciful Jesus, from the treasury of Your mercy You impart Your graces in great abundance to each and all. Receive us into the abode of Your Most Compassionate Heart and never let us escape from it. We beg this of You by that most wondrous love for the heavenly Father with which Your Heart burns so fiercely....

Eternal Father, turn Your merciful gaze upon faithful souls, as upon the inheritance of Your Son. For the sake of His sorrowful Passion, grant them Your blessing and surround them with Your constant protection. Thus may they never fail in love or lose the treasure of the holy faith, but rather, with all the hosts of Angels and Saints, may they glorify Your boundless mercy for endless ages. Amen. (*Diary*, 1215)

Fourth Day

Today bring to Me the pagans and those who do not yet know Me.... (*Diary*, 1216)

Most Compassionate Jesus, You are the Light of the whole world. Receive into the abode of Your Most Compassionate Heart the souls of pagans who as yet do not know You. Let the rays of Your grace enlighten them that they, too, together with us, may extol Your wonderful mercy; and do not let them escape from the abode which is Your Most Compassionate Heart....

Eternal Father, turn Your merciful gaze upon the souls of pagans and of those who as yet do not know You, but who are enclosed in the Most Compassionate Heart of Jesus. Draw them to the light of the Gospel. These souls do not know what great happiness it is to love You. Grant that they, too, may extol the generosity of Your mercy for endless ages. Amen. (*Diary*, 1217)

Fifth Day

Today bring to Me the souls of the heretics and schismatics.... (*Diary*, 1218)

Most Merciful Jesus, Goodness Itself, You do not refuse light to those who seek it of You. Receive into the abode of Your Most Compassionate Heart the souls of heretics and schismatics. Draw them by Your light into the unity of the Church, and do not let them escape from the abode of Your Most Compassionate Heart;

but bring it about that they, too, come to extol the generosity of Your mercy....

Eternal Father, turn Your merciful gaze upon the souls of heretics and schismatics, who have squandered Your blessings and misused Your graces by obstinately persisting in their errors. Do not look upon their errors, but upon the love of Your own Son and upon His bitter Passion, which He underwent for their sake, since they, too, are enclosed in the Most Compassionate Heart of Jesus. Bring it about that they also may glorify Your great mercy for endless ages. Amen. (*Diary*, 1219)

Sixth Day

Today bring to Me the meek and humble souls and the souls of little children.... (*Diary*, 1220)

Most Merciful Jesus, You Yourself have said, "Learn from Me for I am meek and humble of heart." Receive into the abode of Your Most Compassionate Heart all meek and humble souls and the souls of little children. These souls send all heaven into ecstasy and they are the heavenly Father's favorites. They are a sweet-smelling bouquet before the throne of God; God Himself takes delight in their fragrance. These souls have a permanent abode in Your Most Compassionate Heart, O Jesus, and they unceasingly sing out a hymn of love and mercy.... (*Diary*, 1221)

Eternal Father, turn Your merciful gaze upon meek souls and humble souls, and upon the souls of little children who are enfolded in the abode which is the Most Compassionate Heart of Jesus. These souls bear the closest resemblance to Your Son. Their fragrance rises from the earth and reaches Your very throne. Father of mercy and of all goodness, I beg You by the love You bear these souls and by the delight You take in them: Bless the whole world, that all souls together may sing out the praises of Your mercy for endless ages. Amen. (*Diary*, 1223)

Seventh Day

Today bring to Me the souls who especially venerate and glorify My mercy.... (*Diary*, 1224)

Most Merciful Jesus, whose Heart is Love Itself, receive into the abode of Your Most Compassionate Heart the souls of those who particularly extol and venerate the greatness of Your mercy. These souls are mighty with the very power of God Himself. In the midst of all afflictions and adversities they go forward, confident of Your mercy. These souls are united to Jesus and carry all mankind on their shoulders. These souls will not be judged severely, but Your mercy will embrace them as they depart from this life....

Eternal Father, turn your merciful gaze upon the souls who glorify and venerate Your greatest attribute, that of Your fathomless mercy, and who are enclosed in the Most Compassionate Heart of Jesus. These souls are a living Gospel; their hands are full of deeds of mercy, and their spirit, overflowing with joy, sing a canticle of mercy to You, O Most High! I beg You O God: Show them Your mercy according to the hope and trust they have placed in You. Let there be accomplished in them the promise of Jesus, who said to them, I Myself will defend as My own glory, during their lifetime, and especially at the hour of their death, those souls who will venerate My fathomless mercy. (*Diary*, 1225)

Eighth Day

Today bring to Me the souls who are in the prison of Purgatory.... (*Diary*, 1226)

Most Merciful Jesus, Your Yourself have said that You desire mercy; so I bring into the abode of Your Most Compassionate Heart the souls in Purgatory, souls who are very dear to You, and yet, who must make retribution to Your justice. May the streams of Blood and Water which gushed forth from Your Heart put out the flames of purifying fire, that in that place, too, the power of Your mercy may be praised....

Eternal Father, turn Your merciful gaze upon the souls suffering in Purgatory, who are enfolded in the Most Compassionate Heart of Jesus. I beg You, by the sorrowful Passion of Jesus Your Son, and by all the bitterness with which His most sacred Soul was flooded, manifest Your mercy to the souls who are under Your just scrutiny. Look upon them in no other way than through the Wounds of Jesus, Your dearly beloved Son; for we firmly believe that there is no limit to Your goodness and compassion. (*Diary*, 1227)

Ninth Day

Today bring to Me souls who have become lukewarm.... (*Diary*, 1228)

Most compassionate Jesus, You are Compassion Itself. I bring lukewarm souls into the abode of Your Most Compassionate Heart. In this fire of Your pure love let these tepid souls, who, like corpses, filled You with such deep loathing, be once again set aflame. O Most Compassionate Jesus, exercise the omnipotence of Your mercy and draw them into the very ardor of Your love; and bestow upon them the gift of holy love, for nothing is beyond Your power....

Eternal Father, turn Your merciful gaze upon lukewarm souls, who are nonetheless enfolded in the Most Compassionate Heart of Jesus. Father of Mercy, I beg You by the bitter Passion of Your Son and by His three-hour agony on the Cross: Let them, too, glorify the abyss of Your mercy.... (*Diary*, 1229)

APPENDIX D

Indulgences

W hat is an indulgence?

"An indulgence is a remission before God of the temporal punishment due to sins whose guilt has already been forgiven, which the faithful Christian who is duly disposed gains under certain prescribed conditions through the action of the Church which, as the minister of redemption, dispenses and applies with authority the treasury of the satisfactions of Christ and the saints."

"An indulgence is partial or plenary according as it removes either part or all of the temporal punishment due to sin." The faithful can gain indulgences for themselves or apply them to the dead. (CCC 1471)

An indulgence is granted to the Christian faithful who devoutly visit a cemetery and pray, if only silently, for the dead. This indulgence is applicable only to the souls in purgatory. This indulgence is a plenary one, from November 1 through November 8. On other days of the year, it is a partial indulgence.

This indulgence also calls for:

- Reception of sacramental confession.

- Reception of Holy Communion.

- Performance of the prescribed work, such as Stations of the Cross, the Rosary, etc.

- Praying for the pope's intentions — for example, the Our Father, Hail Mary, or any pious prayer.

- That all conditions are met within eight days prior to or after the prescribed work.

What Are Other Devotions That Grant Indulgences?

- Nine First Fridays: For the practice of the Nine First Fridays devotion, Our Lord promises the grace of final repentance.

- Five First Saturdays: For the practice of the Five First Saturdays devotion, Our Lady promises to assist at the hour of death with the graces necessary for salvation.

Moveable Feasts

Holy Thursday

Good Friday

Holy Saturday

Easter Sunday

Solemnity of the Ascension of Our Lord

Solemnity of Pentecost

Solemnity of the Most Holy Trinity

Feast of Corpus Christi or
the Most Holy Body and Blood of Christ

Feast of the Sacred Heart

Feast of the Immaculate Heart

Feast of Christ the King

Feast of the Holy Family

Bibliography and Acknowledgments

Flynn, Vinny. *Mercy's Gaze: 100 Readings from Scripture and the Diary of St. Faustina.* Stockbridge, MA: Marian Press, 2013.

Kosicki, George, W., C.S.B. *Thematic Concordance to the Diary of St. Maria Faustina Kowalska.* Stockbridge, MA: Marian Press, 2015.

———. *Mercy Minutes: Daily Gems of St. Faustina to Transform Your Prayer Life.* Stockbridge, MA: Marian Press, 2006.

———. *Revelations of Divine Mercy: Daily Readings from the Diary of Blessed Faustina Kowalska.* Copyright © 1966 by The Congregation of Marians of the Immaculate Conception of the Blessed Virgin Mary. Ann Arbor, MI: Servant Publications, 1996.

Kowalska, St. Maria Faustina. *Diary of Saint Maria Faustina Kowalska.* Stockbridge, MA: Marian Press, 1987.

Siepak, Sister M. Elzbieta, O.L.M., and Sister M. Nazaria Dlubak, O.L.M. *The Spirituality of St. Faustina.* Krakow, Poland: Misericordia Publications, 2000.

Tarnawska, Maria. *Sister Faustina Kowalska: Her Life and Mission.* Stockbridge, MA: Marian Press, 2000.

Resources

For information about the National Shrine of The Divine Mercy and to become a Friend of Mercy, go to www.thedivinemercy.org.

Association of Marian Helpers
Eden Hill
Stockbridge, MA 01263

Holy Souls Sodality
c/o Association of Marian Helpers
Eden Hill
Stockbridge, MA 01263
www.prayforsouls.org

For memberships and to obtain Masses and Gregorian Masses:

Pious Union of St. Joseph
953 East Michigan Avenue
Grass Lake, MI 49249
(517) 522-8017
www.pusj.org

About the Author

Susan Tassone has long been a passionate champion for the holy souls in purgatory and is recognized as leading a worldwide "purgatory movement."

The award-winning author of eleven best-sellers, including *St. Faustina Prayer Book for Adoration*, Susan makes speaking appearances throughout the country. Over a dozen cardinals and bishops worldwide have endorsed her works. She's a frequent and popular guest on national radio and television programs as well as social media. In 2013, she was featured in the groundbreaking documentary *Purgatory: The Forgotten Church* and was on the cover of *Catholic Digest* magazine in 2017.

She also continues to work tirelessly to raise donations for Masses for the holy souls.

Susan holds a master's degree in religious education from Loyola University Chicago and had the honor and privilege of being granted two private audiences with St. John Paul II, who bestowed a special blessing on her and her ministry for the holy souls.

Learn more at: susantassone.com.

Sophia Institute

Sophia Institute is a nonprofit institution that seeks to nurture the spiritual, moral, and cultural life of souls and to spread the Gospel of Christ in conformity with the authentic teachings of the Roman Catholic Church.

Sophia Institute Press fulfills this mission by offering translations, reprints, and new publications that afford readers a rich source of the enduring wisdom of mankind.

Sophia Institute also operates two popular online Catholic resources: CrisisMagazine.com and CatholicExchange.com.

Crisis Magazine provides insightful cultural analysis that arms readers with the arguments necessary for navigating the ideological and theological minefields of the day. *Catholic Exchange* provides world news from a Catholic perspective as well as daily devotionals and articles that will help you to grow in holiness and live a life consistent with the teachings of the Church.

In 2013, Sophia Institute launched Sophia Institute for Teachers to renew and rebuild Catholic culture through service to Catholic education. With the goal of nurturing the spiritual, moral, and cultural life of souls, and an abiding respect for the role and work of teachers, we strive to provide materials and programs that are at once enlightening to the mind and ennobling to the heart; faithful and complete, as well as useful and practical.

Sophia Institute gratefully recognizes the Solidarity Association for preserving and encouraging the growth of our apostolate over the course of many years. Without their generous and timely support, this book would not be in your hands.

www.SophiaInstitute.com
www.CatholicExchange.com
www.CrisisMagazine.com
www.SophiaInstituteforTeachers.org

Sophia Institute Press® is a registered trademark of Sophia Institute.
Sophia Institute is a tax-exempt institution as defined by the
Internal Revenue Code, Section 501(c)(3). Tax I.D. 22-2548708.